Go Softly !

WWW. SoftskillsHQ. com

270-223-8343

Published by
Robert G. Clark, Publisher
Florence S. Huffman, Editor
Kelly Elliott, Layout & Design
Sid Webb, Cover & Photo Editor

Printed in the USA.

April 2016

First Edition

# Soft Skills Field Manual
## The Unwritten Rules for Succeeding in the Workplace

Greg Coker

# Contents

# How to Get the Most
## out of This Field Manual

This material is a compilation of my work over 25 years in training and development and what I sincerely believe to be the best models, principles and theories on personal and organizational effectiveness. At the end of most chapters are suggestions for internalizing the concepts, questions for consideration and ideas for team activities.

While this Field Manual reinforces and compliments my Soft Skills Boot Camp, these practical, common sense principles, theories and models can be used as a stand-alone resource. My goal is that you will learn more about yourself, your personal style, your strengths, your weaknesses and even your blind spots. This Field Manual is designed for you to learn how to increase personal effectiveness, build teams, and be a more productive member and leader of teams. You will receive tools on how to become a more effective manager, a more inspirational leader, and catalyst for creating and maintaining cultures that engage employees while producing extraordinary results.

Ideally, this Field Manual and workshop experience will serve as an opportunity to "sharpen the saw." Author Steven Covey is famous for a story of two people sawing wood. One, like my late father, was a hard worker rarely stopping for even the smallest of breaks. The second, equally dedicated and committed, factors in breaks, snacks, etc. At the end of the day, who cuts more wood? The second character in the story. Why? Simple, he stopped to sharpen the saw.

This Field Manual is not designed to make you an expert on any given topic. My goal is to simply provide a general overview of the numerous models related to Soft Skills, communication, leadership, and problem solving. While I highlight models, principles and tools designed to enhance personal and organizational effectiveness, it doesn't stop there. No one ever "masters" the Soft Skills; we must commit to continuous improvement, learning from others, trying new things, being open to feedback, and changing as needed.

Before getting started, what specific goals do you have related to enhancing your personal effectiveness? Take a few minutes and list at least three of your goals.

My Personal Goals for Soft Skills Enhancement:

1.

2.

3.

# Dedication

This Field Manual is dedicated to my dad. While he worked hard, he rarely stopped to "sharpen the saw." I miss you dad!

# Introduction

I started my career with a large telecommunications company. We had two divisions in the training organization: Technical Training and Management Training. I was responsible for the latter. Over a 25-year period, I delivered workshops on communication skills, project management, problem solving, and listening skills, to name only a few. I hosted hundreds of management retreats facilitating strategic planning sessions, teambuilding activities and resolving conflict within teams and organizations. In short, I was responsible for developing the "Soft Skills."

I remember my training manager getting upset if she heard anyone refer to what we were doing as "Soft Skills." I'm not so sure why she was offended by that description. Our focus had changed from a "Management Institute" to the "Leadership Institute." We offered programs on teamwork, conflict resolution and culture. We went from screening applicants IQ to encouraging the development of EI (emotional intelligence).

I witnessed firsthand executives in a very technical world hired on their experience only to be fired for their personality. Realizing we had become overly dependent on "Hard Skills," we secured the services of numerous consultants. Warren Bennis, the father of modern management, told us, "Most organizations, including yours, are over-managed and under-led." We were clearly more focused on Technical Skills rather than Soft Skills, on IQ rather than EI.

Times have definitely changed and in survey after survey and conversation after conversation, employers, recruiters, educators and economic developers report workers in all professions and at all levels lack the needed "Soft Skills." These Soft Skills include but not limited to problem solving, conflict resolution, communication, customer service and teamwork.

While not an entirely new term, "Soft Skills" commonly refers to personal attributes that enable one to interact effectively and harmoniously with other people. Soft Skills contrast to Hard or Technical Skills, which are generally more easily quantifiable and measurable. I would be the first to say the "Hard Skills" are the most important. We wouldn't be in business if weren't for the products we produce and the services we provide. But now more than ever, even the most technically focused managers are realizing those products and services are being minimized and slower to market absent the much needed "Soft Skills."

In fact, at a recent conference, the president of one of the Big 3 automotive companies outlined three reasons his company is having difficulty hiring and retaining employees: (1) They can't manage/comply with a basic work schedule (2) They can't/won't show up to work on time and (3) They can't get along with others and work effectively in a team. He said, "While today's employees are technically competent, they often lack the "Soft Skills." They're good at the "What" but no so good with the "Whom."

Unfortunately, it's not just new and entry level employees who lack "Soft Skills." We've all experienced the most seasoned and technically competent employee who may have delivered a product or service but did so in a manner that guaranteed we would never return to that business. Or a co-worker we simply avoid because they lack emotional intelligence and no one wants to be around.

With "Soft Skills" serving as the foundation for my 25-year career and having been exposed to the best models on personal and organizational effectiveness, I naturally felt a responsibility and a calling to provide a solution to what employers were saying was a very serious problem: Employees, new and existing, are lacking the Soft Skills needed for individual and organizational success.

After hundreds of interviews with employers, employees,

students, teachers, economic development professionals and numerous others, three issues emerged:

1. We haven't defined "Soft Skills." Most have a general idea of what is meant by "Soft Skills" but many lack the specifics needed for improvement and performance feedback/coaching.

2. We haven't built the business case for "Soft Skills." Specifically, how much do "Soft Skills" actually benefit organizations? Of course, the next question is – from another perspective – how much is the lack of "Soft Skills" actually costing organizations? Why are "Soft Skills" so important?

3. Most importantly, we haven't trained employees and given them tools that are easy to understand and will enhance "Soft Skills."

## INDIVIDUAL/GROUP ACTIVITY

Individually or in groups of five to six, respond to and discuss the following:

1. How do you define Soft Skills?

2. Do you think Soft Skills are important in the workplace? If your answer is yes, why?

3. Do you think Soft Skills are lacking more today than in the past? If your answer is yes, list the reasons why.

4.   List your Soft Skill strengths.

5.   List your weaknesses related to Soft Skills.

6.   Describe your personal goals to enhance your Soft Skills in the workplace.

# Chapter 1

## Soft Skills: A Working Definition

A compliment to and partner with Technical Skills, Soft Skills are a blend of credibility, likability and most importantly authenticity.

Soft Skills include: Communication, Teamwork, Listening, Problem-Solving, Conflict Resolution, Leadership, Coaching and Emotional Intelligence.

## DISCUSSION

What key words from your definition and/or the working definition grab your attention? Why?

How would you enhance or modify these definitions?

What Soft Skills would you add?

Discuss the differences between Technical Skills and Soft Skills and how they complement each other.

Discuss what it means to be "authentic" and the importance of being authentic.

Describe your organization as related to balancing the Technical versus Hard Skills with Soft Skills.

What changes/modifications do you think need to be made to balance those skills?

# Chapter 2

## The Case for Soft Skills

- The lack of Soft Skills is driving customers, employees, co-workers, students, family members and many others away!
- The lack of Soft Skills is the main drivers for the "drama" in the workplace.
- The lack of Soft Skills is costing billions of dollars per year (absenteeism, management time dealing with personnel issues versus running the business, customer/employee retention, re-training, divorce, fines, hospital visits, incarceration, road rage, etc.).
- The billions invested in programs and initiatives that are quickly diminished or abandoned due to lack of Soft Skills.
- The lack of Soft Skills is the main reason for conflict in teams, organizations, families, and communities.
- In general, our education systems are not teaching Soft Skills; if

they are, these programs are barely scratching the surface with way too much emphasis on theory and not practical application).

- Employees, students, executives and business owners don't understand what is meant by Soft Skills and lack simple and understandable tools to enhance those essential skills.

In our school systems, from kindergarten to college, the lack of Soft Skills may be a contributing factor to the increase in bullying. In a recent school safety study conducted by the Kentucky Office of Education Accountability reports that incidents of public school students accused of bullying, harassing or threatening others has more than tripled since 2012. Unfortunately, the lack of Soft Skills appears to be starting early. Approximately 6,500 violations occurred in elementary schools, 32 percent of the total violations; 59 percent of those violations were from bullying.

In 2015, a Kentucky Chamber of Commerce report surveyed approximately 500 large and small employers asking their opinions of the state's workforce. Twenty-seven percent said they have trouble finding people with good "Soft Skills," which include personal responsibility, communication, and an ability to work well with others. Seventeen percent identified a generational difference in workplace ethics.

While today's employees are technically competent, they often lack what is commonly referred to as "Soft Skills." Work Ready

Skills such as communication, problem solving, customer service, teamwork, and conflict resolution. They leave school knowing "things," but not "people." They're good at the "what" but not so good at the "whom."

In a survey of employers conducted by CareerBuilder, 77 percent said they were seeking candidates with "Soft Skills." Sixteen percent of respondents considered such qualities more crucial than "Hard Skills." A Multi-Generational Job Search Study 2014 by Millennial Branding said employers ranked the following as the most highly desired qualities in candidates: Communication Skills, a Positive Attitude and the Ability to Work in a Team.

The Soft Skills employers are seeking, according to CareerBuilder, Millennial Branding and others, include:

1. Being dependable
2. Having good presentation skills
3. Problem-solving
4. Being able to coach and willing to be coached
5. Fitting into the organizational culture
6. Voicing opinions while being open to feedback
7. Being flexible
8. Focusing on tasks
9. Creativity and innovation
10. Developing new work processes
11. Taking initiative

Soft Skills are Biblical! The "Fruit of the Spirit" is a biblical term that sums up nine attributes of a Christian life according to Paul in his letter to the Galatians, "But the fruit of the Spirit is Love, Joy, Peace, Forbearance, Kindness, Goodness, Faithfulness, Gentleness and Self-Control." Galatians 5:22-23.

Soft Skills is an important economic development tool evidenced by Kentucky's rigorous certification program (Certified Work Ready Community) allowing communities to demonstrate their workforce readiness. This nationally recognized program is an opportunity to differentiate communities within Kentucky and help the state compete to attract jobs. The criteria for Kentucky's "Work Ready Communities" include high school graduation rates, National Career Readiness Certificate holders, community commitment, educational attainment, Soft Skills development and Internet availability.

In fact, Soft Skills are so important to businesses, but unfortunately lacking, many companies (fast food restaurants) are substituting live introductions with a pre-recorded more friendly and upbeat greeting. But what a disappointment when the actual employee follows the pre-recorded greeting with a screeching, "Order when you're ready!"

Perhaps a recent Facebook post said it best:

## 10 SOFT SKILLS THAT REQUIRE ZERO TALENT

1. Being on time
2. Work ethic
3. Effort
4. Body Language
5. Energy
6. Attitude
7. Passion
8. Being coachable
9. Going the extra mile
10. Being prepared

*Author Unknown*

## QUESTIONS FOR DISCUSSION

1. What would you say is the strongest case for Soft Skills?

2. What are examples of programs or initiatives within your organization that have been diminished, thwarted and/or abandoned due to lack of Soft Skills?

3. How could school systems do a better job addressing Soft Skills?

4. Do you think there are generational differences as related to Soft Skills?

5. Is the use of technology enhancing Soft Skills? Diminishing?

6. How could your organization better address Soft Skills?

## SUGGESTIONS FOR ACTION

Survey your employees.

1. How do you define Soft Skills?

2. What Soft Skills are most important in our organization?

3. Which Soft Skills are you most lacking? What is the impact?

4. What are your ideas and suggestions for improving Soft Skills in our organization?

Thank your employees for the feedback, follow-up on the results, implement suggestions, and measure performance.

# Chapter 3

## Building Cathedrals: The Power of Purpose

*If a picture is worth a 1000 words, a metaphor is worth a 1000 pictures.*

My first book, *Building Cathedrals: The Power of Purpose* is based on a story that has been told for over 300 years that demonstrates the most productive and successful people in life and in organizations are those of purpose. And while many have heard a version of this apocryphal story, I discovered the origin of this life-changing story to the world's most famous architect, Christopher Wren. Wren was commissioned to rebuild Saint Paul's Cathedral after the fire of 1666 that devastated London. I revisit the metaphors in this Field Manual because they are powerful, the story applicable and the power of purpose is a key "Soft Skill."

## THE STORY

One day in 1671, Wren observed three bricklayers on a scaffold: one crouched, one half-standing, and one standing very tall, working very hard and fast. To the first bricklayer, Christopher Wren asked the question, "What are you doing?" to which the bricklayer replied, "I'm working, I'm a bricklayer." Totally disengaged.

The second bricklayer, when asked the question, "What are you doing?" responded, "I'm building a wall." Happy about the wall but didn't see the big picture.

The third bricklayer, the most productive of the three, the future leader of the group when asked by Christopher Wren, "What are you doing?" responded with a gleam in his eye, "I'm building a Cathedral to The Almighty!"

## KEY QUESTIONS

1. What is your general reaction to this story? What is its application to you and your organization?

2. Which bricklayer best describes your approach to work? To life?

3. What would you say is the breakdown of "Bricklayers" to "Cathedrals" in your organization? (Percent simply laying brick? Building walls? Building Cathedrals?)

4. Is there a Christopher Wren in your organization? Is it you?

## SUGGESTIONS FOR ACTION

1. Use the bricklayer story in team meetings and planning sessions as an example of the power of purpose.

2. Use "Building Cathedrals" as a theme for a particular organizational initiative.

3. Use the book "Building Cathedrals: The Power of Purpose" for an upcoming conference, book club, or customer appreciation gift. *See page 304 for more information.*

# Chapter 4

## Christopher Wren: Soft Skills Leadership

### *(Leadership is a "Soft Skill")*

In many ways Christopher Wren may have been an ideal leader and the epitome of a Soft Skills practitioner. He was a balanced leader, both left and right brained. Wren was an architect, an engineer and an astronomer—all professions that would have required strong analytical skills to be successful. He was a scientist providing many of the great advances in brain surgery and discovering the importance of antiseptic agents. Wren was an inventor designing military devices as well as machines to lift water, all left-brain or Technical Skills.

But Christopher Wren had many right-brain tendencies as well. His early interest in art, his love of drawing, and the building of several anatomical models for Dr. Thomas Willis, the father of neurology, are clear indicators of strong right-brain tendencies. Additionally, he was a college professor, extremely modest in not seeking credit for his work, and a founding member of The Royal

Society of London. In short, Wren exhibited strong Soft Skills in addition to his technical abilities.

Christopher Wren may have been one of the first and best examples of M.B.W.A., *Management by Walking Around,* clearly a Soft Skill. Imagine Wren at his drafting table looking out over the construction area, grabbing his hard hat, and visiting those who were bringing to fruition his architectural plans. Imagine the reaction of the workers as Christopher Wren visited with each employee. "You know, Wren is the only architect that has ever gotten out from behind his drafting table and spent time with us." Or, "He always asks about my children, he remembers my name, too." Again, the epitome of Soft Skills.

**Employees regularly cite a personal relationship with one's immediate supervisor as the main driver for employee engagement.**

Wren clearly understood and appreciated the difference between management (Technical Skills) and leadership (Soft Skills). Wren was an effective manager as evidenced by the fact that St. Paul's Cathedral is still standing today. There were deadlines and budgets to meet, quality control measures that had to be in place, employees and contractors to be supervised, and regular updates to the City of

London, all very important things managers do. But management is only one component of the equation.

Managers (a Scaffold focus) have to lead as well. Leaders (a Cathedral focus) have to ensure employees see the Cathedral and not just go through the motions, viewing themselves as simply "laying bricks." Leaders have to communicate the mission and vision of the organization. They have to build teams and create cultures for peak performance. They have to be good at the Soft Skills.

Christopher Wren wasn't a flashy or flamboyant leader, the kind we might think of when envisioning power brokers of his time. In fact, research suggests today's great leaders may not fit that profile either. In his bestselling book *Good to Great*, Jim Collins studied companies that made the dramatic leap from simply "good" companies to "great" companies. Collins tracked 11 Fortune 500 companies over a five-year period and coined the term "Level 5 leader" as leaders who blend extreme personal humility with intense professional will.

Level 5 leaders channel their ego needs away from themselves and into the larger goal of building a great company. It's not that Level 5 leaders lack ego or self-interest. Collins suggests they are incredibly ambitious, but their ambition is first and foremost for the institution—for the Cathedral, not themselves. Level 5 leaders model and are heavily dependent on the Soft Skills.

QUESTIONS FOR CONSIDERATION

1. What Soft Skill leadership qualities of Christopher Wren do you find most intriguing? Why?

2. How do you feel Christopher Wren would fare as a modern day leader?

3. What type of culture do you think Christopher Wren would create today?

4. What type of CEO do you think Christopher Wren would be?

5. What can we learn from Christopher Wren as it relates to Soft Skills?

6. Where do you fall in Jim Collins's Level 5 Hierarchy?

   **Level 1:** *Highly Capable Individual:* Makes productive contributions through talent, knowledge, skills, and good work habits.

   **Level 2:** *Contributing Team Member:* Contributes individual capabilities to the achievement of group objectives and works effectively with others in a group setting.

   **Level 3:** *Competent Manager:* Organizes people and resources toward the effective and efficient pursuit of predetermined objectives.

   **Level 4:** *Effective Leader:* Catalyzes commitment to and vigorous pursuit of a clear and compelling vision, stimulating higher performance standards.

**Level 5:** *Executive.* Builds enduring greatness through a paradoxical blend of personal humility and professional will.

7.   Which of the above are Soft Skills? Technical Skills? A combination of the two?

## SUGGESTIONS FOR ACTION

- Select one day a week committed to getting out from behind your desk and simply spending time with your people helping them see the "Cathedral," letting them know how much you appreciate them. Key point: Authenticity.
- While driving down the road (windshield time), simply call your peers, direct reports, family members, and friends simply letting them know how much you appreciate them, love them, etc.
- Leadership by Post-It Note®. Leave a Post-It Note® on someone's desk, windshield, or lunch box to let them know how much you appreciate them, love them, etc.
- Send flowers to a family of an employee you've had on the road or working overtime letting her or him know how much the organization appreciates their support.

# Chapter 5

## The Redemptive Qualities of a Fire

*How one reacts to setbacks (both of their own and of others, both personal and organizational) is a key "Soft Skill." Assisting others through personal fires is also a key "Soft Skill."*

What doesn't kill us makes us stronger. What doesn't turn us into ash turns us into iron. Pre-1666, London was a horrible place. Poverty, prostitution, poor sanitation and 10,000 people dying annually from the plaque. The major contributors to the plague, which had ravaged London for many years, were disease carrying rats and fleas. After the great fire in 1666, the rats and fleas were gone! After the fire, the leaders of London were determined to make London better, stronger and faster. And they succeeded!

While the fire of 1666 was indeed a catastrophic event, there were many positives that resulted from a devastated London. Streets were widened, buildings were rebuilt with less flammable brick and regulations were strengthened. Improvements to sanitation, overcrowding and communication within the city were also made. Additionally, firefighting techniques and strategies were greatly enhanced.

The city that had burned was a medieval one; the London that emerged from its ruins was a modern one. The process of rebuilding began quickly with over 7000 new buildings constructed by 1671. London made a powerful statement to the rest of the world as King Charles II initiated several grand structures demonstrating that the city was indeed back in business. London quickly became the model for modern design with some of America's greatest cities being influenced by the work of Christopher Wren.

## QUESTIONS FOR CONSIDERATION

1. What Soft Skills are needed during a crisis, during a personal "Fire?"

2. What Soft Skills could I deploy to console someone going through a "Fire?"

3. What Soft Skills are needed when organizations are going through "Fires?"

4. How do you typically react during the "Fires" in your life?

5. How does your organization react to the "Fires?"

6. What are your personal "Rats & Fleas?" Organizational "Rats & Fleas?"

# Chapter 6

## A Cathedral: A Personal Expression of Purpose

*Helping others see the big picture and connecting the dots on how what they do supports the building of the "Cathedral," is a key "Soft Skill." Passion for our "Cathedral" is also a key "Soft Skill."*

1. A "Cathedral," is something that adds purpose to our lives, something that drives our behavior. With its stained glass and polished stone each telling a story (and often taken for granted for their beauty), a "Cathedral" is perhaps a perfect metaphor for purpose. Most of us have and can identify with our own personal Cathedral that provides the motivation that keeps us going and working toward something bigger than ourselves. A Cathedral is something that adds purpose to our lives, something that gets us out of bed each morning. A Cathedral

can be something or someone that drives our behavior, our source of energy, and our personal expression of purpose. And, that Cathedral may or may not be able to be built in our 9 to 5 jobs.

Cathedrals come in many shapes and forms. God is The Ultimate Cathedral; our family and our children are primary Cathedrals. Secondary Cathedrals could be our job, a project, an organization, etc. In short, we all need a Cathedral, a purpose, something that keeps us going, something to believe in, and something to build.

## QUESTIONS FOR CONSIDERATION

1. What is your Cathedral?
2. Do you recognize and support other people's "Cathedrals?"
3. Is it time to start building your "Cathedral" or is it time, perhaps, to build with more energy, dedication and purpose?
4. Do you view your organization as a "Cathedral?"
5. Customer loyalty is built at the "Cathedral Builder" level, not at the "Bricklayer" level. Which do your customers see you doing?

**Let your competition "Lay Bricks" while you're "Building Cathedrals."**

# Chapter 7

## Engagement: A Key Soft Skill

The "Bricklayers" in the story provide a backdrop for a rich discussion on employee engagement and the dynamics that occur in modern day organizations.

Like many employees today, the first bricklayer ("I'm laying bricks.") Christopher Wren encountered was clearly "disengaged." A 2011 Employee Engagement Report conducted by the global consulting firm Blessing White found:

- Fewer than one in three employees (31 percent) are engaged and nearly one in five (17 percent) are disengaged.
- More and more employees seem to be looking for a "Cathedral" to build, often outside their current employer.
- Employees view opportunities to apply their talents as top drivers of job satisfaction.

- Trust in executives (the "Christopher Wren" in an organization) can have more than twice the impact on engagement levels than trust in immediate managers. However, employees are more likely to trust their immediate managers than the executives in their organization; reinforcing the need for MBWA (management by walking around) demonstrated by Wren.

- Relationships (Soft Skills) trump technical skills, that is, employees' knowledge of their managers as "people" appears to impact engagement levels more than actions alone.

- Less than two-thirds (61 percent) of respondents say they plan to remain with their organization through the next 12 months.

- Employees flee bad managers (lacking Soft Skills).

The "Christopher Wrens" in our organizations are not immune from disengagement. Top leaders must monitor and manage their engagement, or risk the entire organization suffering, as they tend to be the gatekeepers of the company culture. Many report feeling trapped in leadership roles that no longer provide challenge, meaning, or purpose but given their executive pay, quickly realize they can't afford to leave. Organizations may feel safe now, regarding top management retention, but may be in for a real shock as the economy continues to recover and many top performers leave for opportunities that provide more meaning, more purpose, and maybe for significantly less money. According to the research, less than half of directors and vice presidents are actually engaged.

## QUESTIONS FOR CONSIDERATION

1. Being honest with yourself, with which Bricklayer are you most likely to align?
2. What are reasons for someone viewing themselves as Bricklayers versus Cathedral Builders?
3. What can we do to help others see themselves as Cathedrals?
4. In your organization, do you feel there are more Cathedral Builders or more Bricklayers? Why?
5. How engaged are you? Your employees and team members?
6. What are the key reasons for employee disengagement?
7. How do we get employees engaged?
8. How important is "culture" in your organization?
9. Describe the "Christopher Wrens" in your organization?
10. Describe the "Bricklayers" in your organization.
11. What role do Soft Skills play in employee engagement?

# Chapter 8

## Engagement: The Dynamics Between Two Bricklayers

We can't underestimate the dynamics between two or more bricklayers and the influence they have on each other. In fact, negative workplace relationships may be a big part of why so many employees are not engaged. The first bricklayer in the story is clearly disengaged. Gallop describes these employees as not just simply unhappy at work; they may be busy acting out their unhappiness. Everyday these workers have the potential to undermine what others accomplish.

The second bricklayer in our story could at least "see the wall." Gallop categorizes this bricklayer as "not-engaged." Based on the research, these employees are essentially "checked out." They're sleepwalking through their workday, putting time—but not energy or passion—into their work. But I would be careful of exclusively labeling these bricklayers as "not-engaged." It may be a case of engagement but not on the big picture. Seeing the wall (the trees), but not seeing the "Cathedral" (the forest). Perhaps a case of "tunnel vision." It is important to distinguish between the two.

Gallop analyzed workplace friendships and found that engaged employees are more likely than others to say that their organization "encourages close friendships at work." They found a very close correlation between engaged employees and the relationship with their manager, suggesting that managers who want to boost engagement levels—and help the not-engaged employees become engaged—might benefit from developing trusting and supportive relationships with their employees. Personal relationships (Soft Skills) are a key component to increase employee engagement.

In contrast, actively disengaged employees are especially disenchanted with their connection with their manager. Naturally, engaged employees are much more likely to consider the relationship with their manager to be crucial to success.

Gallop found that of all U.S. workers 18 or older, about 22.5 million—or 17 percent — are actively disengaged; and estimating the lower productivity of actively disengaged workers costs the U.S. economy about $300 billion a year. (Gallop Organization Research Q3 2004)

## QUESTIONS FOR CONSIDERATION

1. What are the dynamics between two or more Bricklayers?

2. What role do you play in assisting that Bricklayer sees the Cathedral?

3. Discuss the differences of the second Bricklayer (one is disengaged and one is focused on the wall). Which one is more prevalent in your organization?

4. How important are friendships in the workplace?

5. How important are the Soft Skills in the workplace?

6. How does the friendship with your boss impact performance? With your direct reports? With your team members?

7. What are some simple steps/activities that could enhance workplace friendships? (employee outings, cookouts, sports, etc.)?

### The Company You Keep

We've heard this from early childhood, "Choose your friends wisely." And it's as relevant now as it was when we were much younger. Hang out with negative people and not only will you be lumped into that category or perception by others in your organization, you'll start thinking like them. At some point, you have to make a stand and remove yourself from the "Bricklayers."

# Chapter 9

## Project 54 Percent - An Opportunity for Engagement

Annual Gallup Polls on employee engagement report that only twenty-nine percent of employees are fully engaged (See the "Cathedral"). Fifty-four percent are partially engaged, building "walls" but not quiet seeing the big picture. The 54 percent are good employees; they're good students. They comply; but are not necessarily committed. They're simply going through the motions. Seventeen percent, based on the Gallup Poll, are disengaged, simply "laying bricks."

The 54 percent may in fact provide the most opportunity and growth for your organization. The 29 percent will be fine. They see the big picture and they're motivated! I'm not suggesting we ignore them. We should be praising them for being in the 29 percent. And rather than wasting their time trying to motivate the motivated, preaching to the choir, we give them the time, tools and incentive to assist us in recruiting the 54 percent. Perhaps we use the 29 percent in assisting in rehabilitating the 17 percent or at least assistance in getting them off the "Bus."

While the 54 percent may provide the most opportunity for cultural transformation, they're also the most vulnerable to be recruited by the 17 percent, who tend to be the most vocal and visible in trying to tear down your organizational "Cathedral." The 17 percent must be dealt with. In fact, this is the "management" part of our job (leadership is what's needed with the 29 percent and the 54 percent.) And the longer we avoid dealing with the 17 percent, the more likelihood the 29 percent and the 54 percent will be negatively impacted (motivation, morale and engagement) by us not addressing poor performance. Unfortunately, the 17 percent is where we spend the majority of our time! At least in the short-term, the 29 percent are able to tune out the interference from the 17 percent. That's not always the case with the 54 percent.

In his book, *Good to Great*, Jim Collins introduces a powerful metaphor, the "Bus." Collins suggests as leaders, we get the right people on the "Bus," (recruitment), the right people in the "Right Seats," (alignment), and the wrong people (the 17 percent I would suggest) off the "Bus." I think most would agree the 29 percent from the Gallup Poll should be on the "Bus." And perhaps a portion of the 54 percent would be in the 29 percent category if they were simply in the "Right Seats." And maybe the 17 percent shouldn't be on the "Bus" at all.

But before we rush to judgment, the majority of the 17 percent didn't show up at your organization in this category (why would you have hired them if they did?). I believe most employees want to build that "Cathedral." But what happens over time—where one slips from the 29 percent to the 54 percent and then to the 17 percent?

I think there are one or two reasons, or maybe both: performance issues and/or a lack of management skills and leadership on our part. For performance issues, management skills (not leadership skills) are needed. With documentation, specifics and attacking the issue (not the person) we address the issue head on. As I mentioned earlier, the longer we delay addressing the poor performers (the 17 percent), the more we risk negatively impacting the 29 percent and 54 percent because not only are they acutely aware of these performance issues but very often are simply waiting for us to deal with them! Address poor performance with clear expectations for 1) changes that must take place; and 2) penalties for not compliance. For the 17 percent, this may be the catalyst to propel them into the 54 percent. If not, we must get them off the "Bus."

I agree with Jim Collins suggestion that every minute we allow a person to hold a seat on the "Bus" when we know they will not make it in the end, we're stealing a portion of his life. This is time that he could spend finding a better place to flourish. Bottom line, we must rehabilitate the 17 percent or get them off the "Bus."

Maybe we haven't addressed the 17 percent hoping it would simply fix itself. Leadership for most is more enjoyable than management, and many have simply stopped managing people. Later in the Field Manual, I introduce the Situational Management/Leadership Model, which says our management and leadership should be determined by the Readiness Level of our employees, and their readiness for a particular task versus our preferred management and leadership style! Unfortunately, many of us are under or over managing or under leading.

## MAJOR DRIVERS FOR EMPLOYEE ENGAGEMENT

1. A personal relationship with one's immediate supervisor
2. Feeling appreciated
3. The opportunity to apply one's skills and talents
4. Friends at work

Perhaps the 17 percent are in this category for one or all of those reasons. The most common remark I hear from managers is, "I've always been told not to get too close to my subordinates and now you're saying that without developing a personal relationship with my direct reports they'll never be fully engaged." That's exactly what I'm saying! Without a personal relationship, you might get compliance (show up on time, leave on time) but not commitment (do whatever it takes). And I'm not talking about after work drinks or weekend golf. Simply caring about your employees as people, spending quality time with them and liking them even though they're not like you! Know their names, their spouses' name, and their children's' names.

Using the metaphors from my book and keynote speech, "Building Cathedrals: The Power of Purpose," you will see across the top three categories: Bricklayer, Wall Builder and Cathedral Builder (see Figure 1).

On the left hand side (*vertically*) list your direct reports. Complete the worksheet by placing an X in the category (Bricklayer, Wall Builder, Cathedral Builder) you think best describes their approach to work.

## ENGAGEMENT

| → | "Brick Layers" | "Wall Builders" | "Cathedral Builders" |
|---|---|---|---|
| Direct Report ↓ | | | |
| | | | |
| | | | |
| | | | |
| | | | |
| | | | |
| | | | |
| | | | |

Figure 1

On the next worksheet and across the top are the following categories: No Relationship, A Basic Working Relationship, and A Close Personal Relationship (see Figure 2).

| Direct Report ⬇ | No Relationship | Basic Working Relationship | Close/Personal Relationship |
|---|---|---|---|
|  |  |  |  |
|  |  |  |  |
|  |  |  |  |

Figure 2

Complete the worksheet by placing an X in the category (No Relationship, A Basic Working Relationship, Close & Personal Relationship) you think best describes your relationship with that particular direct report.

On the next worksheet and across the top are the following categories based on Gallup's percentages related to employee engagement: 17, 54, and 29 percent . . . (see Figure 3). Complete the

# ENGAGEMENT

| ME ➡ | Steps needed to either rehabilitate and/or performance plan or get them off the "bus"? | Steps need to move him/her to the 26%. Steps needed to keep the 19% from recruiting them? | Steps needed to move this person into leadership/more levels of responsibility? How do I prevent burnout and keep them motivated |
|---|---|---|---|
| Direct Report ⬇ | | | |
| | | | |
| | | | |
| | | | |
| | | | |
| | | | |
| | | | |
| | | | |

Figure 3

worksheet by placing an X in the category (17, 54, and 29 percent) you think best describes the engagement level of that particular direct report.

Almost 100 percent of the time, if you view a direct report as a "Cathedral Builder" and in the 29 percent category you report a close personal relationship. The converse is true. If you view a direct report as a "Bricklayer" you will likely report no relationship.

Develop an Action Plan for specific direct reports based on the above worksheets (see Figure 4).

## ENGAGEMENT ACTION PLAN

| Employee | Engagement Strategies<br><br>Steps to Be Taken | Timeline |
|---|---|---|
|  |  |  |
|  |  |  |

Figure 4

## QUESTIONS FOR CONSIDERATION

1. What are your general thoughts about the breakdown on engagement levels (29-54-17 percent)?
2. What are the characteristics of each?
3. How would you approach each?
4. Why do you feel employees are in each?
5. How do we maintain the 29 percent?
6. Is it ok to be in the 54 percent?
7. How do you suggest moving the 54 percent and the 17 percent to the next level?
8. Describe times when you've been in each?
9. Discuss Jim Collins's "Bus" metaphor.
10. How do you most effectively get that person off the "Bus?"
11. What additional reasons for engagement would you add?
12. Discuss compliance versus commitment.
13. Why is a personal relationship with one's immediate supervisor so important?
14. How is this best developed?

# Chapter 10

## What About the Driver of the Bus?

I love Jim Collin's "Bus" metaphor, but there's a key component he doesn't address. What about the "Driver" of the "Bus?" You could have the right people on the "Bus," in the "Right Seats," you have removed the wrong people off the "Bus," but have the wrong "Driver" in the form of a toxic manager. Unfortunately, no one at the top notices the "Driver's" behavior, or worse they turn their heads and ignore the situation because the "Driver" runs an extremely efficient operation (brutally effective) and makes impressive financial contributions to the bottom line.

Everyone on the "Bus" and everyone at the division level are afraid and intimidated to let anyone know about this toxic manager for fear of retaliation. Every messenger has been shot. Revenues are great, the operation appears to be running smoothly, but the "Driver" has created a culture of fear and intimidation with "corporate" simply turning a blind eye to the situation. In short and metaphorically speaking, the toxic "Driver" often leaves causalities behind the "Bus," poisoned by his toxic management.

Operational results and "Technical/Hard Skills" win over culture and "Soft Skills" every time. Management triumphs leadership in most situations with most organizations being "over managed" and "under led." Operations managers (Technical Skills) tend to be promoted over marketing, public affairs or human resources even though the latter disciplines (Soft Skills) may be more suited for leadership. An engineer who is a wonderful operator may not be suited for senior management.

As long as the "Bus" leaves the station on time, arrives at its destination on time, returns, keeps expenses to a minimum and profits high, ignoring the behavior of the "Driver" doesn't seem that big of a risk. But the toxic "Driver" will eventually destroy company culture, profits and employee morale. It is simply unsustainable.

Unfortunately, this also applies to collegiate sports. Former Indiana Basketball Coach Bobby Knight, known for throwing chairs, screaming at players and referees (low "Soft Skills" and low EI-Emotional Intelligence) was quoted after being fired, "I knew once we started losing ballgames, I would be fired." He was right. Many think the university tolerated his "toxic management" way too long. The same could be said about leaders within an organization regarding how long senior management and boards of directors tolerate (or ignore) toxic behavior as a result of outstanding operational results.

How comfortable are you with your organizational "Driving?" Would you be open to placing the following above your office door? How would your employees respond?

## HOW'S MY DRIVING
## CALL 270-223-8343

### QUESTIONS FOR CONSIDERATION

1. What are the characteristics of a "Toxic Driver?"

2. Why do most organizations turn a blind eye to this "Toxic Driver?"

3. Does your organization turn a blind eye?

4. What safeguards can be put in place to prevent "Toxic Drivers?"

5. How should the "Toxic Drivers" be dealt with?

## SUGGESTIONS FOR ACTION

- Consider 360-degree feedback, a system of receiving confidential and anonymous feedback from the people who work around you (direct reports, peers, managers, key stakeholders, to name a few).

- Consider a personal coach as a tool to take your personal effectiveness to the next level.

# Know Thyself

### ~ Plato

# Chapter 11

## Johari Window

The **Johari Window** was created by two psychologists, Joseph Luft (1916–2014) and Harrington Ingham (1914–1995) in 1955 as a technique to help people better understand their relationship with themselves as well as others. There are two key ideas behind the tool:

1. You can build trust with others by disclosing information about yourself.

2. With the help of feedback from others, you can learn about yourself and resolve personal issues.

Across the horizontal axis are *Things I Know* and *Things I Don't Know* (see Figure 1) .

# Things I Know     Things I Don't Know

Figure 1

Down the vertical axis are *Things Others Know* and *Things Others Don't Know* (see Figure 2).

**Things Others Know**

A four-paned "window," as illustrated below, divides personal awareness into four different types represented by four quadrants: Arena, Blind Spot, Closet, and Potential (see Figure 3).

In the first quadrant (*Things I Know; Things Others Know*) is the Arena. The more we can enhance the Arena in our organizations, the closer we move to peak performance. We've all experienced that road trip with others, and as result of being in

**Things Others DON'T Know**

Figure 2

|  | Things I Know | Things I Don't Know |
|---|---|---|
| Things Others Know | ARENA | BLIND SPOT |
| Things Others Don't Know | CLOSET | POTENTIAL |

Figure 3

the car for an extended time, we felt like we got to know each other better. Increasing the Arena makes it easier to demonstrate our "Soft Skills" with knowledge outside of work. For example, ask a co-worker, "How's your band coming along? I remember you telling us about how you played in a Jazz band on most weekends."

How do we increase the Arena? Consider a Monday morning session after a long weekend and before starting the workday, simply get your team together and ask everyone to share what they did over the weekend. It might sound something like this: "Before we get started this morning, let's go around the room and talk about what everyone did this weekend. If you don't have anything or it's still too early, simply say I pass . . . no big deal."

Initially, participation could be an issue. But if you do this on a regular basis, not only will your team grow accustomed to this activity, they will look forward to it! We all have a need for "emotional air" and opportunities like this are too important to pass by. It not only increases the "Arena," it increases productivity and employee engagement.

**Highly effective people are focused on others, are good listeners, and sincerely interested in expanding the Arena through self-disclosure.**

In the second quadrant (*Things I Don't Know; Things Others Know*) is the Blind Spot. We all have blind spots. The key is to solicit feedback on uncovering those blind spots. Do we act upon the feedback? Are we open to the feedback or do we get defensive? Do we make excuses or simply say, "Thank you for the feedback."

The key to giving feedback is making sure it is specific, timely and that it addresses the issue or behavior versus making it personal. And most importantly, the person you're giving feedback must trust you. If not, you're wasting both of your time. If there's trust, there is a good chance they will hear the feedback (it might sting) and act upon your advice or suggestion. If they don't trust you, they will think you're trying to hurt them and take it personally. Without trust, the likelihood of any change in behavior is unlikely.

How do we eliminate the blind spots? If you are sincere and committed to change, simply ask the other person for their feedback. I suggest a private setting and a time convenient for both of you. Perhaps you could call asking them to sit down with you and provide candid feedback. Perhaps, you could sit down over coffee or an afterhours meeting.

In a team setting, it could be a statement that you're committed to being the best you can be and would sincerely like feedback in general or on a particular topic. You're likely to get resistance from certain people who don't feel comfortable delivering this feedback publically. In this setting, you could simply say that you understand this dynamic and that your door is always open for more personal feedback.

Don't be defensive; don't make excuses, thank them for the feedback, act on the feedback, and DON'T SHOOT THE MESSENGER! If you fail to act upon the feedback or shoot the messenger, you'll never get feedback again and your blind spots will continue to exist and expand.

> **Highly effective people have a goal of reducing and/or eliminating Blind Spots. They seek feedback, don't shoot the messenger, and most importantly, act on the feedback.**

The third quadrant (*Things I Know; Things Others Don't Know*) is called the Closet. We all have things we don't feel comfortable sharing with others and this is completely understandable. In fact, we need to understand and appreciate this feeling in others. We also need to understand and appreciate the possibility we make other people feel uncomfortable when we share information that should have been left unsaid.

Certain personalities are more prone to this than others. I have an Expressive personality and my wife often describes me as an "open book." This trait (sharing personal information) can be used to build rapport and trust with others but it can also make some feel uncomfortable. We need to understand, appreciate and respect others' need to keep personal business private, even when we don't completely understand why they hesitate to share details.

**Highly effective people are careful not to make others uncomfortable through inappropriate self-disclosure and/or prying into personal issues.**

The fourth quadrant (*Things I Don't Know; Things Others Don't Know*) is called the Potential. This window receives the least attention but in many ways it's the most important. This is personal and organizational exploration at its best. Perhaps you and others may not have thought you would be good at a particular task, but you take that risk, others take a risk and the "Potential" becomes a reality!

I grew up with a speech impediment and in eighth grade found myself in a speech class. While the speech therapy worked, I was apprehensive to speak publically and lacked confidence. My teacher didn't consider me for her speech team for various and understandable reasons. In fact, my reputation as the class clown probably factored into her perception of me more so than my speaking ability. But a wonderful thing happened. I pushed myself and took a risk. I signed up for the speech team and despite any reservations of my likelihood of success, my teacher took me under her wings. Thanks to the "Potential," I now make a living speaking across the country.

**Highly effective people look for the best in others, push others to be their best, and are open to the possibilities of re-defining both self and others.**

## QUESTIONS FOR CONSIDERATION

1. From a personal perspective, which quadrant do you think has shaped your life?
2. From an organizational perspective, which quadrant do you think has the greatest impact (both positive and negative)?
3. How do you increase the Arena?
4. What strategies do you use in eliminating your Blind Spots?
5. What specific examples do you have related to the power of the Potential?
6. What applications do you see for using the Johari Window?

## SUGGESTED ACTIVITY

Build the Johari Window with your team. Start with the Arena by going around the room and having everyone tell one thing others might not know about them personally. Transition to the Blind Spot by asking for one thing that you suggest the other person consider doing differently (be careful with this portion of the exercise; consider a trained facilitator and establish clear ground rules.) End with the Potential by having those that feel comfortable share an area that would "stretch" them personally or professionally if given the opportunity. Lastly, debrief the activity.

Reference:

Luft, Joseph (1969). "Of Human Interaction," Palo Alto, CA: National Press, 177 pages.

# Chapter 12

## The Appreciation of Differences

In over 25 years in business, I have rarely seen or experienced discrimination in the workplace as related to race, gender, age, national origin or sexual preference. Not that it doesn't exist (unfortunately it does), but I have been blessed not to have experienced or witnessed it. What I have seen and experienced throughout my career is a lack of appreciation of differences on how one generally approaches life. While natural and understandable, assuming others see the world out of the same lens is unrealistic at best and damaging at worst.

We're born with certain personalities. My personality is different than my sister's. Our parents never sat us down and said, "Patty, you're going to be Analytical. Greg, you're going to be Expressive." I didn't set out to meet and marry someone opposite than me but like many couples, it happened (opposites do attract). I didn't intend to place my likes, wants and preferences on my children only to hear, "Dad, I'm not like you!" but it happened. It wasn't my intention to get crossways with my boss because I didn't give him the information and details he needed but it happened, and at the expense of my career with that particular company.

In short, our personalities, our approach to problems and how we view the world varies from person to person. We all bring value to the table. The key is to value both what others and we bring to the table, while understanding and appreciating the differences. If we can harness that diversity, we succeed both individually and organizationally.

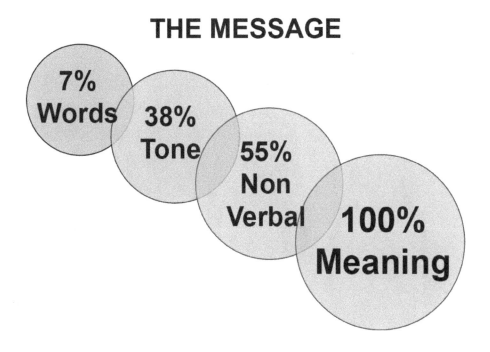

## THE MESSAGE

**YOU ARE THE MESSAGE**

Roger Ailes, nationally acclaimed political consultant, media owner and author, said it best, "You are the Message." Unfortunately, we usually spend more time on "the content" of the message versus the most appropriate delivery method and communication style. And to make communication more challenging, research indicates only seven percent of the message is derived from the actual words we use. The remaining message is from the tone of our voice (38 person) and nonverbal communication (55 person).

## BODY LANGUAGE

According to social psychologist Amy Cuddy, the 55 percent (Nonverbals, specifically Body Language) is a significant predictor in how others see us as well as how we see ourselves. Cuddy suggests "Power Posing" –standing in a posture of confidence even if we don't feel confident–can affect testosterone (dominance hormone) and cortisol (stress hormone) levels in the brain, and might even impact our chances for success . Cuddy's theory is that because our bodies change our minds and our minds change our behaviors, our behavior changes can change our outcomes. Rather than "fake it until you make it," Cuddy suggests we "fake it until you become it!"

Source: *Presence: Bringing Your Boldest Self to Your Biggest Challenges.* by Amy Cuddy, 2015.

## THE USE OF COMMUNICATION MODELS

There have been thousands of books written on communication theory. I've read many of those books and as an undergraduate communication major, the required courses were so academic and boring I routinely questioned my choice of study. It wasn't until I was exposed to numerous communication models did I intuitively understand the communication process. And there's definitely no shortage of communication models and personality profiles out there!

## A FEW ASSUMPTIONS & DANGERS
## OF USING A COMMUNICATION MODEL

The *first* assumption is that as adults we learn from models. While we could describe certain aspects of the communications process, the retention would be minimal without a mental model.

The *second* assumption is that for the most part everything we do, as related to communication, is productive. It's only when we take this asset and use it inappropriately that it becomes a liability.

The *third* assumption is that from a communications perspective we are born with the ability to view the world from basically four windows. While we view the world through all four windows, we tend to look out of one or two more than the others.

The *fourth* assumption relates to the value of building rapport with the one we're attempting to influence. Rapport simply means we like and feel comfortable with people we perceive as similar and with those we feel understand and appreciate us. Having a communication model increases the likelihood that we can predict and match one's preferred mode of communication.

**"All models are dangerous, some are useful."**

The *fifth* assumption is it can be counterproductive and potentially dangerous to label others or yourself with any single model. Individually, our communications patterns are way too complex to be described or explained in any one model. The intent of the Social Style model is to simply add a tool to our communications repertoire, enhancing individual performance and organizational effectiveness. In short, to enhance our Soft Skills.

THE SOCIAL STYLES MODEL

The Social Styles model was designed (Buchholz, Lashbrook & Wenburg, 1976) to measure the assertiveness, responsiveness and versatility of an individual based on perceptions of his communication behaviors. The model is established by looking at two types of behavior. At one end of the spectrum,

Figure 1

the communicator is *task-focused* (see Figure 1). In a team meeting, for example, a supervisor who is task-focused may exhibit this behavior by assertively proclaiming, "Folks, its 8 a.m., let's get started!"

On the other extreme, a team member in the same meeting who tends to be *people-focused* may delay the meeting to allow members and guests to socialize and discuss the weekend's activities. The meeting may not start on time but in her mind the time spent is an investment in the meeting's success. Both styles are effective, just different communication approaches. The challenge is to be in the middle with the flexibility of moving in either direction depending on the situation and the needs of the team or the individual.

Figure 2

On the horizontal axis of the Social Styles model are two additional communications extremes, which complete the model. On the right side is *tell-directed* (see Figure 2). A team member who is more tell-directed may exhibit this behavior by forcefully saying, "We've talked about this for years! We just need to do it and stop studying it!" On the left side of the model, a team member in the same meeting who is more *ask-directed* may exhibit this behavior by raising her hand and saying, "I'm not sure if others feel like I do, but don't you think we've studied this long enough?" Again, both styles are effective, just different approaches. Again, the challenge is

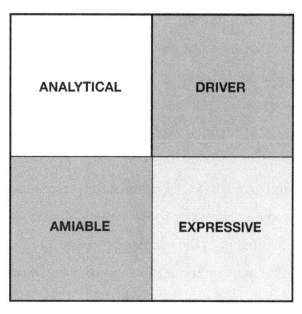

Figure 3

to be in the middle with the flexibility of moving in either direction depending on the situation and the needs of the team or individual.

These four quadrants are the foundation of the Social Styles model (see Figure 3). At the top right, communicators are *task-focused and tell-directed.* Those who look out of this window more than the other three are *Drivers.* Key point: While we look out of all four windows, we typically look out of one or two more than the others. In a presentation (assuming a larger audience with representatives from all four Social Styles, which is typically a safe assumption), target the *Drivers* first! If you fail to do this, *Drivers* will very likely walk out on you (i.e., faking a phone call or restroom break).

When you're communicating with the *Driver*, don't waste time by asking about family or talking about your golf game. Quickly state the purpose for your visit. *Drivers* are more influenced by the "bottom line" and more from what, than from whom.

**Effective communicators customize the delivery of the message based on the communication preferences with whom they are communicating.**

In the top left quadrant are *Analyticals* (task-focused, ask-directed). In a presentation, target the *Analyticals* next (after the Drivers) or risk them mentally checking out (i.e. doodling or daydreaming). When targeting an *Analytical*, slow down your presentation and do your homework. Outline the main points and anticipate the thorough questions. *Analyticals* are influenced by "the research says, or the data suggests." *Analyticals*, like Drivers, are influenced more from what, rather than from whom.

In the bottom right quadrant are *Expressives* (people-focused, tell-directed). With *Expressives*, be excited about your topic, or they'll never completely engage. They typically want to spend more time getting to know you, and are usually animated. *Expressives* readily share information, and are easy to read. They can have short attention spans, and a low need for detail. Provide bullet points speeding up your presentation from your previous meeting with the *Analyticals.* Most *Expressives* would rather slow you down, than speed you up. *Expressives* are influenced more from whom, than from what. Get away from the podium, use gestures, and be excited about your topic. Don't make the *Expressive* wonder if you believe in your topic.

In the bottom left quadrant are *Amiables* (people-focused, ask-directed). Amiables will not be influenced unless you're likeable. *Amiables,* similar to the *Expressives,* are influenced more from whom, than from what. When communicating with an *Amiable,* take your time and be sincere. Personal stories work well with *Amiables.* Arrive early to a meeting and greet as many participants as possible. This personal touch will build rapport with your audience as well as reduce your nervousness once you start your presentation.

For illustration purposes, the following model separates the Social Styles model into two segments: Driver/Analytical and Expressive/Amiable (see Figure 4).

**DRIVER/ANALYTICAL**
Credibility
IQ
Management
Brain
Logic
Organization
Scaffold
RFP

**EXPRESSIVE/AMIABLE**
Likeability
EQ
Leadership
Heart
Faith
Culture
Cathedral
Closing the Deal

Figure 4

- The top part of the model (Driver/Analytical) is "Credibility" while the bottom part (Expressive/Amiable) is "Likeability."
- The top part of the model is "IQ," the bottom is "EI."
- Top part of the model is "Management," the bottom is "Leadership."

- Top part the "Brain," the bottom is the "Heart."
- Top part "Logic," the bottom part is "Faith."
- Top part "Organization," the bottom part is "Culture."
- Top part is the "Scaffold," the bottom part is the "Cathedral."
- Top part "RFP," the bottom part is "Closing the Deal."

## YOUR NEXT PRESENTATION

1. Target *Drivers* first by clearly stating the purpose of your presentation. If you fail to do this, expect an exodus of people faking phone calls, restroom breaks, etc.

2. Slow the presentation down and hit the *Analyticals* next with a well-organized, systematic and logical outline.

3. For *Expressives*, pick it up and show excitement for the topic outlining "impact" and "significance." You should consider adding graphics, animation, and music

4. Build rapport with *Amiables* by being likable. Personal stories with authentic and heartfelt emotions when and where appropriate.

Interestingly, many marketing materials follow this sequencing of communication. Enter USA Today. The first section is a bullet-pointed highlight of the day's news (*Driver*). Second, the Money section (*Analyticals*). Third Sports (*Expressives*) and fourth, the Life section (*Amiables*).

Colleges and universities profile the quick facts regarding graduating rates and tuition costs. (*Drivers*) on page one of a brochure. Page two is more detail about admission standards, information needed for tuition assistance (*Analyticals*). Page three highlights sports teams, excitement on campus (*Expressives*), ending with a professor and her students on the university lawn experiencing a close-up and personal lecture (*Amiable*).

## ASSUMPTIONS ABSENT INFORMATION ABOUT YOUR AUDIENCE

*(Presentations should include all four Social Style quadrants, but depending on the audience one` or two quadrants could dominate.)*

- Early morning meetings: Primary focus on Drivers/Analyticals
- Evening presentations: Primary focus on Expressives/Amiables
- Business Groups: Driver/Analyticals
- Technical Groups: Analyticals
- Educators: Expressive/Amiables
- Sales/Marketing: Expressives/Amiables
- Younger audiences: Expressives/Amiables

## STRESS SHOWS IN COMMUNICATION

Each Social Style quadrant has a *"Back-Up"* behavior that appears during stressful situations. Under normal conditions, we operate out of our preferred and dominant style, an effective mode of communication. However, under stress we go to a *"Back-Up"* response mode. Back-up modes are unproductive at best and often destructive. Individuals who habitually operate in Back-Up mode are *"unemployable."* Politicians who habitually operate in Back-Up mode are *"unelectable."* Employees who habitually operate in Back-Up mode are at best *"ineffective"* and at worst will sabotage an organization's bottom line. Soft Skills are rarely present but often needed when operating in one's Back-Up mode.

**The lack of Soft Skills is often a contributing factor (if not *the* contributing factor) for stress and resorting to "Back-Up" mode!**

There are four Back-up modes or styles: Autocratic, Withdraw, Attack, and Acquiesce.

The Back-Up mode of *Driver* is *Autocratic (see Figure 5).* Common phrases used to describe *Drivers* who are operating out of their Back-Up mode are *"Autocratic," "Dictatorial,"* or *"My way or the highway."*

# Back-Up Behaviors

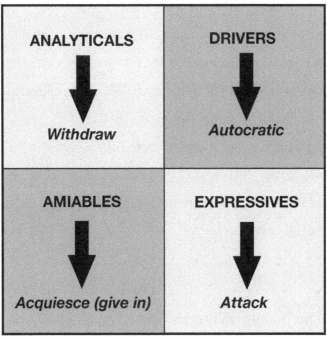

Figure 5

The Back-Up mode of the *Analytical* is to *Withdraw.* Common phrases used to describe *Analyticals* who are operating out of the Back-Up mode are *"I'll take my ball and go home"* or *"Hide out in my office."*

The Back-Up mode of the *Expressive* is *Attack.* If a fellow co-worker has ever snapped and sworn at you, he or she was most likely an *Expressive.* The Back-Up mode of the *Amiable* is *Acquiesce* (give-in). Common phrases used to describe an Amiable who operates out of their Back-Up mode are *"Wishy Washy" and/or "Always gives in."*

The value of being aware of one's Back-Up mode is the ability to monitor both individual behavior as well as recognizing when others are under stressful conditions. Ideally, we operate in our *"normal"* communication mode most of the time. When we experience stress and go to our Back-Up mode, we recognize this shift and do whatever possible to get back to our normal, more productive communication style. Unfortunately, this doesn't always happen. A third part of the *Social Styles* model is a phenomenon called *"Z-ing Out,"* which should be avoided at all costs!

## Z-ING OUT

*"Z-ing Out"* occurs while under stress and we cannot/do not get back to our normal, more productive style of communication, we travel from one *"Back-Up"* mode to another. The *Driver* under stress goes to his/her Back-Up of *Autocratic (see Figure 6).* If they cannot get back to their normal *Driver* style, he will move over to the "Back-Up" of the *Analytical,* which is to *"Withdraw."* At this point, if they cannot recognize they are under stress and move back to their normal style of communication—they will go to the *Expressives* "Back-Up" mode and *"Attack."* The Z is completed as the *Driver* then heads to the "Back-Up" of the *Amiable* and *Acquiesces.*

An example of a *Driver* "Z-ing Out" was Richard Nixon during

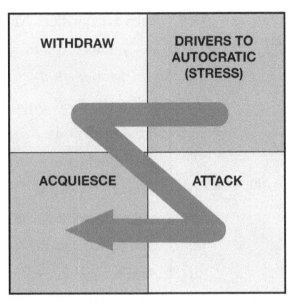

Figure 6

the 70s Watergate crisis. Nixon became *"Autocratic"* demanding key staff to engage in illegal activity only later to *"Withdraw"* to Camp David. Nixon eventually began his *"Attack"* by blaming liberals, communists and Democrats. Nixon completed his "Z" by resigning *(Acquiesce)*.

Many feel Bill Clinton demonstrated the "Z-ing Out" pattern during the Monica Lewinski scandal. Bill Clinton, the *"Driver"* became *"Autocratic"* by controlling all data and accounts of his relationship with Lewinski. Like Nixon, he retreated to Camp David and actually traveled abroad more frequently than before *(Withdraw)*. Predictably, Clinton and his staff started their *"Attack"* on Ken Starr, the Republicans and the vast "Right Wing Conspiracy." As only Clinton could do, he cheated the Social Styles model and *"sort of" "Acquiesced"* by going on national TV and saying, "I did have a relationship with that woman." A full-scale *"Acquiesce"* would have

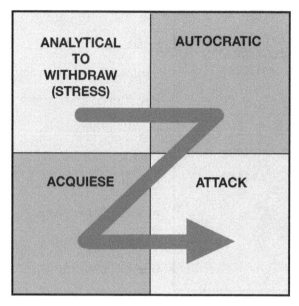

Figure 7

been a resignation. Not in Clinton's playbook.

The *Analytical's* back-up is *"Withdraw."* If the Analytical cannot reduce her stress and return to a normal mode of communication, the *Analytical* will travel across the Social Styles model to *"Autocratic" (with their data)* then down to *"Acquiesce"* completing the *"Z-ing Out"* pattern with *"Attack"* (see Figure 7). An example would be the financial team member attempting to persuade an organization that the "numbers don't add up" and under stress *"hides"* in his office *(Withdraw).* They eventually emerge becoming *"Autocratic"* with their many reports. After failing to convince the decision makers, the Analytical throws their hands up saying, "go ahead, and take this company down the tubes" *(Acquiesce)* only later to reappear and *Attack* by saying "I told you so."

The *Expressives* back-up mode is *"Attack."* After the *"Attack" (usually verbal)* the Expressive will realize how bad they've just screwed up and apologize *(Acquiesce).* If the other person will not accept the apology, the *Expressive* will then become *"Autocratic"* by making a case of how they're not appreciated and no one understands, etc. *Expressives* will then leave the scene

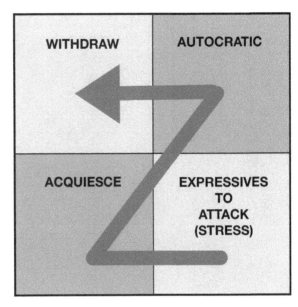

Figure 8

*(Withdraw). Expressives* will not stay away long as they love a good fight (Figure 8). Expressives under stress are usually "all bark and no bite."

*Amiables* back-up mode is to *"Acquiesce."* The three other styles *(Driver, Analytical and Expressive)* have the ability to recognize when they are in "Back-Up" mode and exhibit the proper "stress management" and return to normal communication. While the *Amiable* may recognize they're *"Z-ing Out",* they reach a "point of no return" very quickly in the process. An *Amiable* will give in and give in and give in and give in *(Acquiesce).* But run for the hills when the *Amiable* starts *"Z-ing Out"* (see Figure 9).

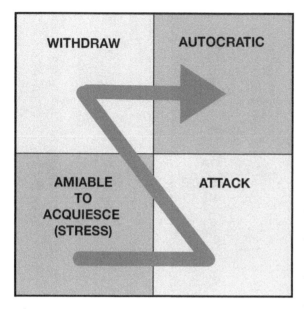

Figure 9

The *Amiable* "Attacks" (uncharacteristic for the *Amiable*) and then *"Withdraws."* The final *"Z-ing Out"* phase for the Amiable is to become *"Autocratic"* by controlling the relationship. While the *Expressive* under stress attacks with more bark than bite, the *Amiable* growls and growls and growls but when they bite, it is vicious!

## VERSATILITY

While no one would suggest an *Analytical* attempt to be an *Expressive* or a *Driver* try to become an *Amiable*, the communication challenge is *Style Versatility*. *Style Versatility* is a reflection of a person's willingness to adapt and cope with a variety of individuals and situations without sacrificing his/her own personal communication style. In short, "If your favorite tool is a hammer, be careful not to treat everyone else like a nail." Remember. *"You are the Message."*

**Soft Skills & Versatility go "hand in hand!"**

IN THE MIDDLE

The challenge is to be in the middle of the Social Style Model (Figure 10). The goal is communication balance allowing movement from one style to another natural and comfortable.

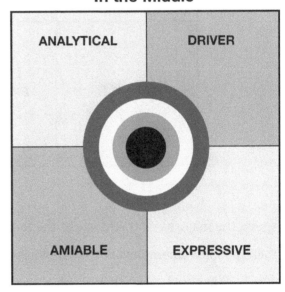

Figure 10

AVOIDING THE FOUR CORNERS

If you're in one of the four corners, even communicating within that quadrant will be a challenge (too analytical for other *Analyticals*) and nearly impossible to communicate effectively with those in the other quadrants. (Figure 11) Unfortunately, we all know those who

## Avoiding the Corners

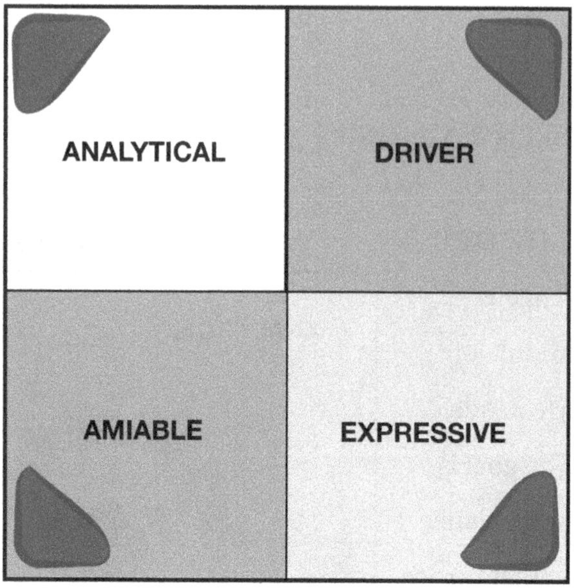

Figure 11

spend the majority of their lives in the four corners. What do you call these people? Unemployable, incarcerated, unproductive, unelectable, expelled, habitual "performance plan" participants, etc.

## YOU ARE THE MESSAGE

- Your Smile is your *Logo.*
- Your Personality is your *Business Card.*
- How you leave others feeling after an encounter is your *Trademark.*

## QUESTIONS FOR CONSIDERATION

1.  Which style best describes you?
2.  What would you consider to be your strengths related to your preferred style?
3.  Weaknesses?
4.  Which style drives you crazy? Why?
5.  What could you learn from that style if you could better understand and appreciate it?
6.  What is the predominate style in your workplace? How does that style help? Hurt?
7.  What is the least dominant style in your workplace? What is the impact?
8.  Describe times when you go to your "Back-Up"? Cause? Effect? How do you prevent it?
9.  Describe when others go to their "Back-Up?" Cause? Effect?
10. What is the impact of "Z'ing Out" in the workplace? At home?
11. How does one achieve balance and stay in the middle?
12. Have you ever been "Credible" at the expense of being "Likeable?"
13. What about "Likeable" at the expense of being "Credible?"
14. Does your organization's marketing materials factor in unique communication needs and styles of target audience(s)?

## You Never Get a Second Chance to Make a First Impression

Harvard Business School professor Amy Cuddy has been studying first impressions for more than 15 years, and has discovered patterns in these interactions.

In her book, *Presence*, Cuddy says people quickly answer two questions when they first meet you:

- Can I trust this person?
- Can I respect this person?

Psychologists refer to these dimensions as *warmth* (Soft Skills) and *competence* (Hard Skills) respectively, and ideally you want to be perceived as having both.

Interestingly, Cuddy says that most people, especially in a business, believe that competence is the more important factor. After all, they want to prove that they are smart and talented enough to handle your professional needs.

But in fact warmth, or trustworthiness, is the most important factor in how people evaluate you. "From an evolutionary perspective," Cuddy says, "it is more crucial to our survival to know whether a person deserves our trust." It makes sense when you consider that in cavemen days it was more important to figure out if your fellow man was going to kill you and steal all your possessions than if he was competent enough to build a good fire.

While competence is highly valued, Cuddy says it is evaluated only after trust is established. And focusing too much on displaying your strength can backfire.

Cuddy says certain business people are often so concerned about coming across as smart and competent that it can lead them to skip social events, not ask for help, and generally come off as unapproachable.

These overachievers are in for a rude awakening when they're not considered for career enhancing opportunities because nobody got to know and trust them as people.

"If someone you're trying to influence doesn't trust you, you're not going to get very far; in fact, you might even elicit suspicion because you come across as manipulative," Cuddy says.

"A warm, trustworthy person who is also strong elicits admiration, but only after you've established trust does your strength become a gift rather than a threat."

## DON'T IMMEDIATELY WRITE THEM OFF

Certain personalities take longer than others to develop lasting relationships. Give it time; don't give up, in most cases it will be worth it. However, certain people you will never be able to develop a relationship. It's them, not you. Move on.

# Chapter 13

## Stress Management

Armed with the sharpest Soft Skills tools, they still may be insufficient during stressful situations. In fact, sometimes our worst emerges during stressful situations. As described in the previous chapter, each style has a "Back-Up" during stress. The key is recognizing when we're under stress, understanding behaviors most likely to emerge during stressful situations, avoiding those behaviors if possible, and returning to our most productive communication style.

While stress can be personally managed, we often find ourselves needing assistance from a professional. Such was the case when I had gone through one of life's most stressful events, a job loss. As we had coffee, Skip Wirth in his most supportive and enthusiastic voice said, "Greg, you're going to come through this!" He continued, "You have the seven characteristics of stress resistant people." In his signature rapid-fire approach, Skip outlined all seven characteristics. What follows is a summary of that conversation.

## All Stressed Up and No Place to Go

### By Skip Wirth

For over 36 years, stress, its effects on the body and life management skills for mediating the harmful effects of chronic stress, has been my passion. Throughout the years, I have spoken to well over 1000 audiences on some form of this topic, and for good reason. Stress is now recognized as the number one killer. This is not the world according to Skip; this comes from the American Medical Association. In fact, the American Institute of Stress estimates that 90 percent of all visits to doctors are for stress-related disorders. How can this be? Have you ever picked up your newspaper and read a headline stating, "Another Person Killed by Stress"? Not likely. Stress is a killer by proxy and is behind the five leading causes of death in America.

Several weeks following September 11, 2001, I was invited to be the guest speaker for a Chamber of Commerce. I eagerly accepted the offer, but my thoughts quickly turned to, "What can I say to this group that will help to lift their spirits, give them hope, and help them to reclaim those parts of their lives that have them spinning out of control?" America was still hurting, my audience was still hurting. The memories of that horrible day still haunted them. My speech, "All Stressed Up and No Place to Go" was written precisely for this occasion. In essence, it is an overview of seven characteristics of stress resistance people. Much credit goes to Dr. Raymond B. Flannery, Jr. who authored the book, *Becoming Stress Resistant,* a must read!

We all know people who just seem to glide through life. Even though they encounter difficult life circumstances, they always bounce back. What do they have that others don't? If they have it, can we have it also? How much of it do we need? Is it possible to incorporate what they do into our lives and become more like them? YES!

In studying these individuals, researchers such as Dr. Flannery, Dr. Herbert Benson and Hans Selye, among many others, have identified characteristics these people have in common that make them less vulnerable to the harmful effects of stress, characteristics that add years to your life and life to your years.

The seven characteristics of stress resistant people are as follows:

1. *Stress resistant people take personal control.* When confronted with a problem or stressor, these people take charge. They take self-initiated, self-directed problem solving strategies to resolve the problem. They don't roll over and wait for others to come to their rescue. They are empowered, not overpowered. They know

what personal resources are available to them and they bring them to bear. After the horror of 9/11, feelings of being out of control were pervasive. However, those feelings were replaced with planned, organized and self-directed strategies to rebuild.

2. *Stress resistant people are task involved.* All of us need a reason to live. A purpose in life. A task that we are personally or existentially committed to. Examples of task involvement include our families, jobs, church activities, hobbies, volunteer projects, and our pets. We need to feel like we matter, that we make a difference. We know it as self-esteem. We strive to become valued partners in our life's journey. Have you noticed that when a person retires from work but fails to fill that once occupied space with something meaningful, they often wither and die? Boredom is a very powerful, negative life force and is best avoided. The German philosopher Nietzsche wrote, "A person with a *'why'* to live for can bear most any *'how.'*

3. *Stress resistant people seek social support.* We need each other, and this need is biologically rooted. You may tell yourself, "If it weren't for all of these people I would feel more sane." Quite the opposite is true. Research shows that people with few or no close contacts die at higher rates for every major cause of death. Recently, chronic loneliness was risk-equated to a one pack per day smoking habit. If you are a lonely smoker, you are in deep

doo! Just for a moment, reflect on all the helpful social exchanges in your life: love, affection, trust, respect, support, empathy, nurturing, dignity, appreciation, listening, caring and bonding, just to name a handful. We need each other!

4. *Stress resistant people make wise lifestyle choices.* This is where the rubber meets the road. Mark Twain wrote, "The only way to keep your health is to eat what you don't want, drink what you do not like, and do what you'd rather not." Unfortunately, far too many Americans subscribe to that notion. In 2001, the Centers for Disease Control (CDC) reported that only one fourth of American adults exercised enough in the 1990s. Only 25.4 percent of adults met government recommendations for physical activity. Nearly 30 percent reported no physical activity at all (except for blinking and clicking). The CDC recommends 30 minutes of moderate exercise, like walking, five times a week, or 20 minutes of vigorous exercise such as running, cycling, rowing or swimming, three times a week. The 30-minute requirement can be broken into chunks as small as 10 minutes, with everyday activities like gardening. Walking may be the perfect exercise. "Regular physical activity such as walking is probably as close to a magic bullet as we will come in modern medicine," said Dr. JoAnn Manson, Chief of Preventative Medicine at Harvard's Brigham and Women's Hospital. "If everyone in the U.S. were to

walk briskly 30 minutes a day, we could cut the incidence of many chronic diseases 30 to 40 percent." Modifications in lifestyle could prevent or delay 75 percent of illness and disease. This is startling! What comprises the remaining 25 percent? Genetics, for which you have no control over, and environment, for which you have very little control over. That 75 percent modification in lifestyle is a large, powerful stick for which you have complete control! Just for clarity, lifestyle encompasses your diet, exercise, stress management, sleep, safety (do you wear seat belts?), substance use/abuse (smoking, excessive alcohol, drug abuse), as well as other lifestyle factors.

5. *Stress resistant people have a sense of humor.* When I was young, I remember hearing on a television variety show that, "Laughter is the best medicine." I remember thinking that sounded great, but how do they know that? Do doctors prescribe laughter for their patients? Sure, laughter felt good like a warm blanket, but the best medicine? In recent years, a great deal of scientific evidence supports that assertion. Humor and laughter stimulate the immune system, lowers blood pressure, increases endorphin levels (the hormone that makes you feel good), decreases stress, helps oxygen to be utilized more efficiently, and helps to control pain. Too bad we can't put humor in a pill form and bottle it! Researchers discovered that on average, toddlers laugh 400 times

a day. Adults laugh only 15 times a day. My first impression, "What a rip-off! What price am I paying by giving up 385 laughs a day?" Actually, my laughing habits are more like the toddlers. Researchers also found that anger (opposite of happiness) triples mortality rates, and that whining, which is anger through a smaller opening, has similar consequences.

6. *Stress resistant people espouse religious values and have an ethical regard for others.* This probably comes as no surprise to most of you, even in our "get ahead at any cost," competitive environment. All of the great religions of the world say the same thing: love your neighbor. You remember the Golden Rule— do unto others. Dust it off because it still applies in a deep and visceral way. Studies show that religious people tend to live healthier lives. "They are less likely to smoke, to drink, to drink and drive," says Harold Koenig, M.D., Associate Professor of Medicine at Duke. In fact, people who pray tend to get sick less often, as separate studies at Duke, Dartmouth and Yale Universities reveal. Some statistics from these studies:

   • Hospitalized people who never attended church have an average stay of three times longer than people who attended regularly.

   • Heart patients were 14 times more likely to die following surgery if they did not participate in a religion.

- Elderly people who never or rarely attended church had a stroke rate double that of people who attended regularly.
- In Israel, religious people had a 40 percent lower death rate from cardiovascular disease and cancer.

Also, says Koenig, "People who are more religious tend to become depressed less often. And when they do become depressed, they recover quickly from depression. That has consequences for their physical health and the quality of their lives." What goes on in our head is powerful medicine indeed!

7. *Stress resistant people are optimistic.* I am fortunate because I inherited this one from my mother. Throughout my youth and adulthood, she was the epitome of optimism—light, cheery, funny, and encouraging. She was one of life's cheerleaders. Optimism, a close cousin to happiness, protects the heart and lungs, boosts the immune system, reinforces self-esteem and helps reduce long-term stress. Studies now prove that happy people are "more likely to get and stay married, have friends and participate in organizations," says Sonja Lyubomitsky, from the University of California at Riverside. "They are more likely to pursue goals, more energetic, more likely to be hired and less likely to be fired." "Optimism is a frame for how you view the world and happiness is an emotion," explains Harvard University's Laura Kubzanksy. Just 10 percent of happiness

comes from individual circumstances, 50 percent from genetic inheritance and 40 percent is uncharted. Do you know how to tell the difference between an optimist and a pessimist? An optimist wakes up in the morning and proclaims, "God, it's a good morning!" A pessimist wakes up in the morning and grunts, "Good God, its morning!" Same morning—different view.

These seven characteristics are not unlike ingredients to a wonderful recipe. Incorporate these ingredients into your life and something wonderful transforms — YOU! In order to make these ingredients easier to remember, I have repackaged them into "Skipisms" that I call "The Seven F's,"

- Faith
- Family
- Friends
- Food
- Fun
- Fitness
- Focus

What a recipe for life! Bon Appetit!

Vincent "Skip" Wirth has over 35 years of experience as a teacher, trainer, speaker and coach and has conducted over 1500 workshops regionally and nationally on stress management, wellness, fitness, communication, team building, leadership, customer service, marketing, motivation and humor in the workplace. His effectiveness is born out of a strong sense of purpose, principle and ethics as well as his commitment to excellence. Skip is a Registered Nurse and has over 38 years of health care experience including clinical, supervisory, education, sales, marketing, and administration. Contact Skip today for your keynote, training and coaching needs. www.skipwirth.com

## QUESTIONS FOR CONSIDERATION

1. Out of the seven characteristics, which are the strongest for you? Weakest?
2. What characteristics would you add to Skip Wirth's list?
3. What are the major causes of stress in the workplace? Personally?
4. What impact does stress have on you in the workplace? Personally?
5. How do you minimize and deal with stress in your life?

## PUT THE GLASS DOWN

A psychologist walked into a room, where she was teaching stress management to an audience. As she raised a glass of water, everyone expected they'd be asked the "half empty or half full" question. Instead, with a smile on her face, she inquired: "How heavy is this glass of water?"

Answers ranged from 8 oz. to 20 oz.

She replied, "The absolute weight doesn't matter. It depends on how long I hold it. If I hold it for a minute, it's not a problem. If I hold it for an hour, I'll have an ache in my arm. If I hold it for a day, my arm will feel numb and paralyzed. In each case, the weight of the glass doesn't change, but the longer I hold it, the heavier it becomes."

She continued, "The stresses and worries in life are just like that glass of water. Think about them for a while and nothing happens. Think about them a bit longer and they begin to hurt. And if you think about them all day long, you will feel paralyzed-incapable of doing anything."

Remember to put the glass down.

# Chapter 14

## Emotional Intelligence

## EMOTIONAL INTELLIGENCE: HOW WE HANDLE OUR RELATIONSHIPS AND OURSELVES

Our emotions are contagious and play a crucial role in our personal effectiveness and success. If we resonate energy and enthusiasm, our effectiveness and success will be enhanced.

The converse is true. If we spread negativity, mistrust, fear, and intimidation, our effectiveness and success will be diminished. We excel not just through our *"Skills & Smarts,"* but how we *"Connect"* with others.

In The Emotional Intelligence Quick Book, authors Travis Bradberry and Jean Greaves describe four main components of Emotional Intelligence:

- Self-Awareness (Helpful tools: Social Style Model, Johari Window, feedback from others);

- Self-Management (Keeping your emotions in check, managing negative behavior, operating from dominant Social Style versus "Back-Up" and not Z-ing out);

- Social Awareness (Awareness of cliques, your effect on others, team/organization dynamics, increasing the Arena); and

- Relationship Management (Aware of and commitment to repairing broken relationships. Recognizing and appreciating others, developing new relationships, maintaining current ones, and reconnecting with old ones).

From both a life and organizational perspective, Emotional Intelligence is changing our concept of "being smart." Emotional Intelligence (EI) how we handle ourselves and our relationships— coupled with our intelligence, determine life and career success. We've all witnessed someone with an extremely high IQ coupled with low EI crash and burn. Sadly, many are hired on their expertise only later to be fired on their personality and lack of "Soft Skills." In the sports world, there are many examples of a winning coach fired after numerous self-destructive incidents and low EI behavior.

## LIKEABLE AND CREDIBLE

Politically, many candidates are recruited based on their resume and defeated as a result of not connecting with voters, or worse, they're simply unlikable. From a non-partisan observation, Hillary Clinton is perceived as unlikable, hence the book by Edward Klein titled, "Unlikeable." Former president Bill Clinton on the other hand was and is perceived to be very likeable and credible. Former president George Bush (43) is perceived as likeable but not always credible. Ronald Reagan joins Bill Clinton, in my opinion, as both likeable and credible.

## ENGAGEMENT

We follow leaders with whom we connect. In fact, numerous Gallup Polls cite the number one reason for employee engagement is a personal relationship with one's immediate supervisor, a supervisor with high EI that recognizes the link between relationship and performance. Unfortunately, our view of human intelligence has been narrowly focused, often ignoring a crucial range of abilities that matter immensely in terms of success in our business and personal lives. Emotional Intelligence may explain why people of high IQ flounder and those of modest IQ coupled with high EI do surprisingly well.

## EI AND JOB TITLE

Travis Bradberry and Jean Greaves in *The Emotional Intelligence Quick Book*, make the connection between EI and job title. Their findings are both surprising and alarming. They found that EI scores rise from front-line supervisors to middle management, but beyond middle management, there is a steep decline in EI scores. For the titles of director and above, scores sharply decline with CEOs on average having the lowest EI scores explaining the earlier statement, "Many CEOs are hired on their expertise and fired on their personality."

## BE HERE NOW: YOUR LISTENING SKILLS

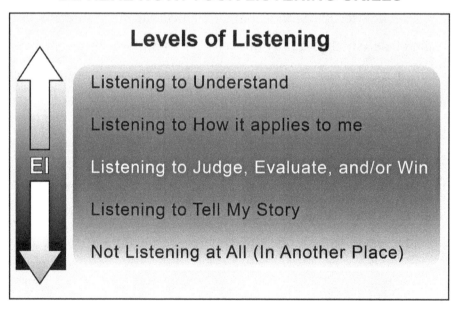

**Levels of Listening**

EI

Listening to Understand

Listening to How it applies to me

Listening to Judge, Evaluate, and/or Win

Listening to Tell My Story

Not Listening at All (In Another Place)

## QUESTIONS FOR CONSIDERATION

1. How would you rate your EI? Others EI in your organization?

2. List what you feel are key components of EI?

3. How can EI be developed and strengthened?

4. What is the impact of high EI in the workplace?

5. What is the impact of low EI in the workplace?

6. Which does your organization value most? Explain.

7. What is the relationship between Soft Skills and EI?

8. What does EI do the further you move up the organizational chart?

# Chapter 15

## Forgive and Reconcile

I first met Dan Cherry when he was Secretary of the Kentucky Justice Cabinet when I conducted a team-building workshop for then Governor Paul Patton and his executive cabinet. Dan Cherry is like most heroes, you would have never known of this legend by his quiet demeanor and humble spirit. But it didn't take long to realize Dan Cherry was and is to this day an amazing man. Brigadier General Dan Cherry, USAF, (Ret.) served our country for 29 years, flying airplanes such as the F-105, the F-4 and the F-16. He also commanded the Air Force Thunderbirds, the 8th Tactical Fighter Wing and the Air Force Recruiting Service.

On April 16, 1972, then Major Dan Cherry was on a mission near Hanoi, North Vietnam, when he encountered a dogfight that would change his life. Major Cherry squeezed the trigger of his radar guided AIM-7 Sparrow missile hitting a North Vietnamese MiG-21 jet, which exploded in a huge fireball. The MiG pilot ejected and his parachute opened directly in front of Major Cherry. Dan Cherry continued to serve his country many years after that eventful day over North Vietnam.

Dan Cherry had a dream of a park in his hometown of Bowling Green, Kentucky, that would honor local pilots who had made significant contributions to aviation. But little did Dan Cherry realize this particular project would change his life and the lives of many others in ways no one could have ever imagined. And that's the beauty of purpose. When we pursue our passions, we usually find that in addition to our lives being forever altered, other's lives will be significantly changed as well.

Dan Cherry and a group of his walking buddies took a trip to the National Museum of the United States Air Force in Dayton, Ohio. The one exhibit that changed lives that day wasn't even at the museum. Knowing that Dan Cherry and his friends were from Kentucky, a staff member commented about an airplane that held some historical significance to the Bluegrass state. He told them it might become available because the VFW where it was located was having difficulty taking care of it. As fate would have it, that VFW was only 20 miles down the road. To everyone's amazement, the numbering 66-7550 on the tail of the F-4 Phantom jet left no doubt that Major Dan Cherry had been reunited with an old friend from 30 years earlier.

Dan Cherry's F-4 Phantom jet soon had a new home in Bowling Green and it became clear that the seed of an idea planted with the discovery of that plane had flowered into something much bigger than anyone had ever imagined. Today, the Aviation Heritage Park honors some of America's finest combat aviators and there are plans to host many more airplanes and honor the pilots who flew these magnificent machines.

"For over 30 years, I filed away memories of that MiG pilot that I shot down," recalls Dan Cherry. "Did he have a family? Did he survive the bailout and return to fly again?" Curious, Dan Cherry wrote a letter to a journalist and TV show anchor in Vietnam and only a few weeks later, Dan Cherry received an invitation to appear on the show, "The Separation Never Seems to Have Existed."

Thirty-years after that life-changing dogfight, Dan Cherry would meet Nyugen Hong My, the pilot of the defeated MiG 21. Since then the two men have become close friends, spending time together both in Vietnam and in the United States. The power of forgiveness and reconciliation prompted Nyugen Hong My to ask Dan Cherry to research the American pilot that the Vietnamese pilot had shot down. Dan Cherry kept his promise and on April 26, 2009, Nyugen Hong My and the American he shot down embraced each other with tears in their eyes as Steve Hartman of CBS News expressed, "the war went away."

Dan Cherry went on to write *My Enemy, My Friend* that is a must read. Proceeds from the sale of his book go to the Aviation Heritage Park in Bowling Green, Kentucky. To purchase your copy, visit: www. aviationheritagepark.com today!

## THE LACK OF FORGIVENESS AND RECONCILIATION IN THE WORKPLACE

During my career, I have worked for three fortune 500 companies, served as a government regulator, both as a private and public school board member, a board member of numerous nonprofit organizations as well as a consultant to hundreds of businesses in the areas of leadership, team building, and organizational development. Most of these companies have one thing in common: Performance has been significantly throttled by a lack of forgiveness and reconciliation between employees, managers, board members, community leaders, business owners, and regulators.

Hundreds of examples exist of the lack of forgiveness and reconciliation preventing both individuals and their organizations achieving maximum potential. Consider the public utility and city commission that are at odds with each other over every issue – due to the president of that utility and a council member's interpersonal conflict dating back 30 years. What about two co-workers who haven't spoken in months for reasons they can't even remember. Worse still, two siblings who allow a difference of opinion to divide a family until it's too late.

After delivering a keynote speech to an organization with all its employees in attendance, the president invited me to return the next morning for a debrief with her management team. We started by going around the room having each participant share one or two learning points they felt had significant application to the organization.

While most responses centered on leadership, team effectiveness and customer service, one senior manager stated the need for forgiveness and reconciliation in the workplace had the most impact on him. Then something amazing happened: He started to cry as he turned to the gentleman sitting next to him and said, "It's time we move on my friend." They embraced and it was like a terminal cancer had left the organization! Privately, the president commented, "I couldn't believe they were even sitting next to each other first of all and I still can't believe what happened after that!"

## FORGIVENESS IS A CHOICE; NOT AN EMOTION. RECONCILIATION DOESN'T NECESSARILY MEAN RESOLUTION.

Forgiveness is a choice; not an emotion. If we wait until we "feel" like forgiving someone, we'll likely never do it. But after we finally "choose" to forgive, why don't we reconcile? Most think reconciliation requires resolving the issue. And it doesn't.

In fact, when I'm asked to do a workshop for an intact group I have participants raise their right hand and repeat after me, "I promise that when a team member with whom I need to reconcile calls me for a coke next week, we will not discuss the crap! We're simply moving on!"

## STILL CARRYING AROUND YOUR ROCK? IT MAY BE SMALLER, BUT IT'S STILL A ROCK!

One Sunday as I walked into a church service, I was handed a small rock about the size of a half-dollar, one that you would find in a creek bed. The message was John 8:7 (those without sin throw the first stone). At the end of the service, our minister suggested if we were withholding forgiveness from anyone (family member, friend, co-worker, former boss), today was an opportunity to place your rock on the altar. He invited us to walk down to the altar and although many went down, I didn't because I felt I had pretty much forgiven the only person I needed to forgive (key words: pretty much). But on occasion I still think about the past (that's the devil working). So basically, the "rock" I'm carrying may be smaller (I don't hate him as much...) but it's still weighting me down. The following day, as I was driving down the road, that little rock, which had been so heavy for so long, finally flew out the window. What about your rock?

## QUESTIONS FOR CONSIDERATION

1. What is the impact of lack of forgiveness and reconciliation in the workplace?
2. Is there someone needing your forgiveness?
3. Why is forgiveness important?
4. Is there someone with whom you need to reconcile?
5. What is the impact of not reconciling?
6. Could you perhaps be a catalyst, a facilitator in helping others start the forgiveness and reconciliation process?
7. Why is not discussing the "Crap" so important?
8. What action steps are necessary to accomplish forgiveness and reconciliation?
9. Are you still carrying your rock? A little one? A big one?

*"Spread love everywhere you go: First of all in your own house. Give love to your children, to your wife or husband, to a next-door neighbor... Let no one ever come to you without leaving better and happier. Be the living expression of God's kindness; kindness in your face, kindness in your eyes, kindness in your smile, kindness in your warm greeting."*

~ Blessed Mother Teresa of Calcutta

# Chapter 16

## Coaching

There are no shortages of coaching models and like most things: we make it harder than it has to be. Ironically, coaching is not what we see most "coaches" doing. Screaming and yelling high school football plays on a Friday night is not the best coaching model in the workplace. The original model of coaching is perhaps better suited than modern day definitions.

### ORIGINAL COACHING DEFINED

A vehicle designed to take passengers from where they are to where they want to go.

Many of us have a personal coach, whether formal or informal. In times of crisis, we reach out to

those we trust and who provide honest feedback in a constructive and non-judgmental manner. That was the case when I transitioned from 25 years in corporate America and started my training and consulting business. I reached out and found a performance coach who assisted me in getting from where I was to where I wanted to be.

There's a difference between "Directing" and "Coaching." Many report "Coaching" an employee, coworker or family member, when in reality they're directing. And "Directing" is appropriate in many situations. If there's one characteristic of an effective coach it's listening more than talking. In fact, if you find yourself doing most of the talking and giving directions, you're probably not coaching.

In my workshops, I have participants pair up and practice coaching. We record the sessions having participants count the numbers of seconds each speak. Inevitably, the one who is supposedly "Coaching" talks more than the one he or she is coaching. Additionally, if the "coach" finds herself attempting to solve the problem versus facilitating the problem solving, they're probably managing versus coaching.

**Sometimes we need someone to simply be there. Not to fix anything, or to do anything in particular, but just to let us feel that we are cared for and supported.**

**~Unknown (but everyone)**

## REMOVING INTERFERENCE

I first met Alan Fine when he worked with our company's senior management team. Alan is a former professional tennis coach turned leadership and organizational development coach. He is the author of *"You Already Know How to Be Great: A Simple Way To Remove Interference And Unlock Your Greatest Potential."* After a few hours in the classroom, he took our entire team out to the tennis court and one at a time started hitting balls across the net to us.

As you can imagine, most of our management team were not the best tennis players. I had actually played competitive tennis but was rusty at best. As each volleyed with Allen, tennis balls were flying everywhere. Clearly, we were embarrassed with our poor performance and preoccupied with how we looked in front of our peers. In short, interference (embarrassment and peer pressure) was preventing acceptable performance. To add to my embarrassment, Alan asked if I would join him in a demonstration.

After volleying for a few minutes, Alan started asking questions. "Greg, what do you notice?" "I notice I'm hitting these balls all over the place," I responded. "When do you notice this," Alan asked. "As soon as I hit the ball," I barked. Alan: "Tell me what you notice when you hit the ball?" I responded, "I notice that fuzzy yellow missile coming over the net." Tell me more about that fuzzy yellow missile," asked Alan. "I notice the letter P (Penn: the brand of ball) coming at me," I yelled! "Tell me more about that P," said Alan. I reply, "I see it tuning over and over."

After numerous questions from Alan, all based on what I was focused on, amazingly my returns started going over the net versus over the fence. I was actually volleying with a professional tennis coach! Alan Fine demonstrated the negative impact interference was having on my performance. Most importantly, he modeled how effective coaching can assist in eliminating interference, eventually improving performance.

Alan never screamed, "Greg, you can do better!" or, "It's your grip. Now let's go back over everything I've told you!" The traditional model of coaching is to increase knowledge. Conventional thinking, if you want to get better, is to read a book, attend a workshop, or hire an expert. This approach assumes people are lacking in some area and that more knowledge is the answer to improve performance. And there are times when additional knowledge will enhance performance.

But if this were the case in every situation, reading a book or attending a workshop would improve performance every time. We would all be incredible leaders, the best parents and the club champions! Allen Fine suggests the biggest obstacle in performance is not knowing what to do, it's not doing what we know. In short, it's not about knowledge acquisition, it's about execution.

When Allen and I were volleying, I knew how to hit a tennis ball. Interference (embarrassment and peer pressure) prevented me from doing what I knew how to do. In short, an effective coach assists in identifying interference and coming up with methods of reducing and/or eliminating that interference thereby increasing performance.

I've been a golfer most of my adult life and at one point was consistently shooting in the low 80s. But I could never seem to break 80. There were hundreds of times I was on my way to shoot in the 70s only to choke with an out of bounds ball or three putt on the last few holes. I would tense up and listen to that inner voice telling me I wasn't capable of shooting a 78 or 79 or letting my buddies rattle me. Although I read numerous books on golf and spent thousands of dollars on golf lessons, I never broke 80.

But then, twice on the same course I shot a 78! Every shot was crisp. I didn't have to think about anything! It felt effortless. My mind was quiet, my muscles relaxed. I experienced what professional athletes call "Flow." My performance was less about adding new knowledge and more about eliminating interference that was getting in the way of implementing the knowledge and skills I already had!

If it's a lack of knowledge with a subordinate, teaching and directing may be more appropriate than coaching. And unlike coaching, this would be more of "taking a person from where they are to where *you* want or need them to go."

**H**

| COACH DRIVEN (Not Bad) | EMPLOYEE DRIVEN (Ideal) |
|---|---|
| COACH/MANAGER DRIVEN (Not Good) | COACH/MANAGER DRIVEN (Not Good) |

Willingness to Engage

**L**     **Awareness of Issue**     **H**

## COACHING

Helping the other person determine where they want to go, removing interference, and assisting them in getting to their desired destination.

## THE ROLE OF TRUST

There must be trust between you and the person you're coaching or you're both wasting your time. Without trust, the person you're trying to coach may likely think you're trying to hurt them. Directing would be a more effective approach, with compliance being the outcome versus commitment usually associated with and the result of coaching.

## GREG COKER COACHING MODEL

**Step 1:** Determine trust level. No trust, no coaching.

**Step 2:** Determine willingness to be coached. (This is assuming you've approached the person to be coached. If the one you're coaching approached you, trust is assumed.)

To be "Coachable," GiveMore.com, suggests the person we're coaching should:

1. Be approachable
2. Be attentive
3. Be receptive
4. Be curious
5. Be objective
6. Be trusting
7. Be shapeable
8. Be grateful

A quick five-point checklist on one's "Coachability." Which of these statements are true for the person you're considering coaching, and to what extent?

1. They usually allow others to complete their sentences before responding. If yes, "Coachable." If not, re-assess.

2. When given feedback or constructive criticism, they usually think about it for a few moments before responding rather than immediately defending their position or action. If yes, "Coachable." If not, re-assess.

3. When given feedback or constructive criticism, they usually ask in-depth questions in order to better understand. If yes, "Coachable." If not, re-assess.

4. Over the last year, they've changed a position or approach to a situation because of advice from another individual. If yes, "Coachable." If not, re-assess.

Ideally, the person you're coaching will be in the top two quadrants. If they're in the bottom two quadrants, re-assess coaching.

### BE HERE NOW

As a coach, it is important to be willing to dedicate 100 percent of your time and attention to the coaching session. Turn off your computer, forward your calls, close the door, and avoid glancing at your smartphone or android device. If you cannot "Be Here Now," re-schedule the coaching session.

**Step 3:** Start with three basic questions:

- What's going well?
- Where are you getting stuck?
- What will you do differently moving forward?

Assuming this is a new experience, it may take a few times before the one being coached and perhaps even you feel completely comfortable. Be prepared for the one being coached to immediately start with "Where I'm getting stuck" versus "What's going well." Don't give in; insist on starting with "What's going well?"

## POOP SANDWICH

It will take time to erase the "Poop Sandwich" culture from the performance appraisals at your organization. A "Poop Sandwich" is where the manager gives the employee a little positive, followed by the negative, then ending the session with a little more positive. If managers do this on a regular basis, no one will ever hear the positive because they anticipate what's going to follow – they will be thinking about what just happened at the same time you're delivering the positive feedback (usually at the end of this less than effective performance appraisal).

## A COACHING SESSION

Coach: Will, thanks for coming in. Let me join you over there at the conference table. (In a coaching session, it is important to remove all physical barriers, like a desk in this example.) Important note: If there's a serious performance issue where you want to establish who's in charge, sitting behind the desk would subtly and nonverbally communicate this authority (this would probably not be a coaching session.)

Coach: Will, I appreciate your willingness and trust in seeing me as a source of feedback and coaching.

Will: I appreciate your time. I've been here two years and love my job. Overall, I feel pretty good about where I am. There are times however I feel my direct reports aren't responding to my leadership. Could you give me your honest opinion on what you think I might be doing wrong?

Coach: Will, you know I'm always here for you. To get started, I would like to ask you a few questions. First, what's going well? And, do you mind if I take notes just for this conversation? Also, let's keep this coaching session issue specific versus personal if at all possible.

*Reminder: As a coach, you should be talking less than the person you're coaching.*

Will: I'm fine with you taking notes. And, I will keep it issue specific. I really don't have an issue with any particular person.

*Important note: If there are personal issues, be extremely careful not to take sides. Coach Will on how he might improve his relationship with that other person versus making comments about the person with whom Will has an issue. Encourage Will to go directly to that person.*

Will: I just feel like when I try to communicate with my folks they don't always take me seriously.

Coach: Will, let's start with what's going well. You said overall you feel pretty good with your effectiveness and I hear good things about you from all departments. So tell me what's going well.

Will: (He outlines several areas where he feels that's going well.)

Coach: Great list, Will. I would add a few if you would be open to hear them.

Will: Sure!

Coach: (Coach outlines a few areas where he feels Will is doing well and asks Will if he has questions regarding those items.)

Coach: Will, you want to move to the "getting stuck?"

Will: Yes. Where do you think I'm getting stuck?

Coach: Will, assuming you feel there may be areas that you're getting stuck, where do you think those areas might be? And again, I'm going to jot these down just to aid our conversation. I will destroy my notes once we're through.

*Reminder: Again, it's natural for the one you're coaching to want you to provide the responses.*

Will: (He outlines a few areas…at times he starts to go too deep in one area.)

Coach: Will, let's get them all listed first and then you can clarify and provide additional information if needed.

Will: (He lists four or five areas where he feels he's getting stuck.)

Coach: (Coach asks a few clarification questions, asks for specifics.)

Will: (He provides clarification.)

Coach: Will, I have an idea you might consider. Would you be interested in hearing my perception? (*If the Coach doesn't have anything to add, simply say, "Will, I don't have anything to add."*)

Will: Definitely!

Coach: (Coach outlines a few items being as specific as possible, factual versus emotional and asks Will for any clarification he may need.)

Coach: Will, I've written down the areas in bullet point form that you've identified and I've added where you might be getting stuck. Pull your seat around here and let's review.

Coach: Will, what do you think about maybe brainstorming a few action items that might assist in getting you "unstuck" if you will?

Will: I think that would be a good idea.

Coach: Ok, I'm going to give you a few minutes to list options on what you could do to eliminate or minimize these situations where you think you're getting stuck. (It's important to give Will quiet time so he doesn't feel rushed with the Coach standing over him. Also, encourage brainstorming anything, as crazy as it might seem, that might be on the table. The Coach may leave the room for five minutes or so.)

Coach: Ok, Will, are you ready to review your list?

Will: Yes!

(3) Get Commitment to pursue identified items

Coach: Let's look at the list first and then we can discuss specific items you would be interested in pursuing.

Will: Ok. Here they are.

Coach: Good list. Do you know which one has top priority? Obviously, there are a few you probably don't want to pursue (with brainstorming and because you encourage anything goes, there will probably be a few that are more realistic than others). Will, can you identify which ones you want to pursue?

Will: (Will identifies three items he would like to pursue.)

Coach: Will, specifically what will item number two look like once you've completed it? How will you know you've been successful? (Coach presses for measurable specifics on each item.

Will: (Will provides more specifics while the Coach writes all of this down.)

Coach: Are you satisfied with the list, Will?

Will: Yes, I really am!

**Step 4:** Get Commitment regarding timeframes on agreed upon Action Items

Coach: Excellent! Let's put these three items on an Action Plan.

## Action Plan

| WHAT | WHO | WHEN |
|------|-----|------|
| Employee Retreat/ Team Building | Will/ Team | 10-1 |
| Employee Survey | Will to Coordinate | 5-1 |
| Leadership Training | Will to Investigate Options | 4-1 |

**Step 5:** Establish/Get Commitment on the Follow-Up

Coach: So, Will, when I call you on (see WHEN on Action Plan), tell me what you plan to accomplish? (Will describes particular items.) (Coach needs to follow up with Will on this particular date.)

Will: Thanks!

**Step 6:** Debrief Coaching Session

Coach: You're welcome, Will. Let's debrief our time together. Overall, what went well? Anything you or I could have done differently?

**Step 7:** Follow-Up with Will on the agreed upon date.

# Chapter 17

## Yes, Everyone Really Does Hate Performance Reviews

This article appeared in the Wall Street Journal on April 11, 2010. It was written by Samuel A. Culbert, author of *"Get Rid of the Performance Review! How Companies Can Stop Intimidating, Start Managing – and Focus on What Really Matters."*

It's time to finally put the performance review out of its misery.

This corporate sham is one of the most insidious, most damaging, and yet most ubiquitous of corporate activities. Everybody does it, and almost everyone who's evaluated hates it. It's a pretentious, bogus practice that produces absolutely nothing that any thinking executive should call a corporate plus.

And yet few people do anything to kill it. Well, it's time they did.

Don't get me wrong: Reviewing performance is good; it should happen every day. But employees need evaluations they can believe, not the fraudulent ones they receive. They need evaluations that are dictated by need, not a date on the calendar. They need evaluations that make them strive to improve, not pretend they are perfect.

## WHO, ME?

Sadly, most managers are oblivious to the havoc they wreak with performance reviews. To some extent, they don't know any better: This is how performance reviews have been done, and this is how they will be done. Period.

Here's a simple experiment you can try. Ask yourself: How often have you heard a manager say, "Here is what I believe," followed by, "Now tell me, what do you think?" and actually mean it? Rarely, I bet.

The performance review is the primary tool for reinforcing this sorry state. Performance reviews instill feelings of being dominated. They send employees the message that the boss's opinion of their performance is the key determinant of pay, assignment, and career progress. And while that opinion pretends to be objective, it is no such thing. Think about it: If performance reviews are so objective, why is it that so many people get totally different ratings simply by switching bosses?

No, instead, the overriding message is that the boss's assessment is really about whether the boss "likes" you, whether he or she feels "comfortable" with you. None of this is good for the company unless the boss is some kind of savant genius who can read an employee's talents with laser accuracy—and then understands what motivates the employee so perfectly that he or she can push just the right psychological buttons to get the employee to use those talents.

Unlikely and even more unlikely.

## THE DAMAGE DONE

At this point, you may be asking: So what? So what if you can't speak your mind to your boss? So what if the performance review forces the boss to focus on an employee's "weaknesses" (since most bosses are told they can't give *everyone* top grades)? What harm does it really do?

Sadly, it does enormous damage. Forget, for a minute, the damage it does on a personal level—the way it makes work lives miserable, the way it leaves employees feeling depressed and anxious, the way having to show so much tolerance at work leaves them with too little tolerance at home. Just think about what it does on a corporate level, the enormous amount of time and energy it wastes, and the way it prevents companies from tapping the innovative, outside-the-box thinking that so many employees are capable of. If only, that is, they weren't so afraid.

## A BETTER WAY

The good news is that none of this is the way things have to be. The one-sided, boss-dominated performance review needs to be replaced by a straight-talking relationship where the focus is on results, not personality, and where the boss is held accountable for the success of the subordinate (instead of just using the performance review to blame the subordinate for any problems they're having).

In this new system, managers will stop labeling people "good guys" and "bad guys"—or, in the sick parlance of performance reviews, outstanding performers, average performers, and poor performers to be put on notice. Instead, they'll get it straight that their job is to make everyone reporting to them good guys.

If you're a boss, and your subordinate isn't succeeding, something is broken here. Doing more of the same isn't going to cut it. It's now time for you to ask, "What do you need from me to deliver what we are both on the firing line to produce?" And just as important, it's time for you to listen to the answer.

Asking and listening. Imagine that. It's called a conversation, and it's a rarity in workplaces today. Only by hearing what the other person thinks, and putting that person's actions in the appropriate context, can you actually see what the person is saying and doing—and how together you can get where the company needs you to go

Performance reviews won't get you there, because that's just about the boss getting the subordinate to buy into his or her way of thinking. It's a mirror—not a window into the other person. But take away the performance review and you might actually have straight talk.

## ROTTEN MILK

Proponents of performance reviews say that the problem isn't the review itself, but poorly trained reviewers. Sorry, but that doesn't fly: The performance review done exactly as intended is just as horribly flawed as the review done "poorly." You can't bake a great cake with rotten milk, no matter how skilled the chef. They also say you need performance reviews to protect against lawsuits by laid-off workers. Nonsense: Most performance reviews *hurt* a company's case because they aren't honest assessments of a worker's performance.

Also, before you start griping about how I don't understand Margaret, the woman in your department who wants to do as little work as possible, or how Tom is so distracted by his life outside the office that he can't get anything done at work, let me stop you and say: I know that not *everybody* deserves to stay in their jobs. Getting rid of performance reviews doesn't get rid of slackers. Not everybody will leap at the chance to get better and grow.

But *everybody* deserves the best shot managers can give them. And they can't get that shot with performance reviews.

## QUESTIONS FOR CONSIDERATION

1. What are your general thoughts about coaching?
2. How does coaching differ from directing?
3. What is the value of coaching?
4. Who would you consider to be the best coaches?
5. What characteristics do they all have?
6. What is the value of "Be Here Now?"
7. What are the potential pitfalls of coaching?
8. What do you consider to be the most important steps in coaching?
9. What are your general thoughts about performance appraisals?
10. Ever have a "Poop Sandwich?"
11. Are performance appraisals in your organizations a positive experience?
12. If not, what improvements would you suggest?

# Chapter 18

## Change

### SEVEN DYNAMICS OF CHANGE

There's no shortage of commentary, theory and models related to change both in the workplace and in our personal lives. Organizationally, they range from Kurt Lewin's popular Unfreeze-Change-Refreeze Model to the ADKAR Model (Awareness, Desire, Knowledge, Ability, Reinforcement).

Personally, they range from Elizabeth Kubler-Ross's Stages of Change (adapted from her Stages of Grief) to Stephen Covey's Seven Habits model, originally published in *The Seven Habits of Highly Effective People,* challenging us to examine our values and the way we react to change in our lives.

Conceptually, we understand change. As leaders we preach the need for change and its importance. We quote phrases like "The only constant is change," and covet buzzwords like "Change Agent." We read the latest books on change and listen to podcasts and attend workshops on this popular topic.

But until we've been at the receiving end of change, we'll never fully understand or appreciate the true dynamics of change. My first job was in training and development where I taught numerous classes on change management. In theory, I understood the need for change and the significance of both organizational and personal change. I was young and resilient.

And like many organizations in the early nineties, our company experienced "downsizing." I distributed our propaganda and assured restless employees our outplacement services would be available and of value during their transition. I preached courage, resiliency and the dangers of making the company one's identity. I was indeed a "Change Agent."

But it wasn't until I was at the receiving end of change that I truly understood and appreciated the dynamics of change. One afternoon as I checked the mailbox and saw a package addressed to: William Gregory Coker-Employee 42134270. Intuitively, I knew I was definitely at the receiving end of "real" change. I had been identified as a candidate for the "downsizing" I had so eloquently preached.

Again, until you've been at the receiving end of "real" change, you really don't understand the dynamics of change. The following exercise makes powerful learning points regarding change in the workplace while serving as an energizing activity. This exercise works with both large (I've used it with over 100 during conference) and small groups (for best results, the group should be no smaller than 20).

## DIRECTIONS

1. Make a general statement about change in organizations. How we've all read books, magazine articles, heard speeches on change. But until we're at the receiving end of change, we really don't understand the dynamics of change. And before we implement change, we should be cognizant of the impact it has on those going through a particular change. Clearly state the goal of this exercise: To place participants at the receiving end of change, making the debrief more personal and less academic.

2. Direct everyone to standup and find a partner (threesome is ok if there's an odd number). Turn so you are facing your partner face-to-face. For the next 30 seconds, no talking! Your task is to simply observe the personal appearance of your partner(s). Emphasize "No Talking!"

3. Repeat the instructions several times within the 30 seconds. The goal is to make participants feel uncomfortable. Extend the time by counting out loud. "Only 20 more seconds left…18, 17, 16… Longest 30 seconds of your life!" The volume of your instructions will be important, as the room will be loud with talking and laughter.

4.  After 30 long, drawn out seconds, announce: "Now, turn so that you are back-to-back with your partner. I want you to change three things in your personal appearance." Be very very specific with these instructions. Make sure you say "change three things" and not "take 3 things off." This will be a key point during the debrief. Repeat directions several times. I will also say, "Once you make a change, keep it changed until I say the exercise is over." Some participants will be freaking out having to change just three things. Some will be having a ball, laughing and not concerned with changing three things. Make note of these dynamics for the debrief (without embarrassing anyone or calling anyone by name).

5.  After a few minutes, say: "Now, turn around so that you are face-to-face with your partner." Direct them to "Identify the three things that have changed." Again, remind them to keep the changes in place until the exercise is over. Most will be laughing and having a fun at this stage of the exercise. I usually give participants a few minutes to identify the changes.

6.  "Ok, now turn so that you are back-to-back with your partner again. This time I want you to change five additional things in your personal appearance, eight things total!" Many are starting to freak at this point. You will hear comments like, "I don't have enough clothes on!" Repeat instructions, "Change

five additional things in your personal appearance." Again, make note of the dynamics.

7. After a few minutes, have participants turn back around and face their partner and identify the five additional changes. Most will be laughing at the crazy things changed (mostly clothes, belts, shoes, etc. that have been taken off).

8. After a few minutes direct everyone to once again turn where they are back-to-back with their partner(s). "Now, change five additional things." You will barely get these words out and participants will be ready to kill you! You've made the necessary points and say something like, "Ok, I sense a little resistance! Let's sit down and talk about what just happened." Most will be laughing and putting things back on, finding their seats.

9. Once everyone has settled down and back in their seats, repeat the fact that we could have talked about change and it would have been academic. But this exercise was designed to place participants at the receiving end of change so we could debrief the dynamics of change both from one who is at the receiving end of change (employee) and from one who is leading the change (manager).

10. Debrief the Seven Dynamics of Change. I typically go over these pretty quickly and then after I have covered all seven with a brief explanation after each one, I will open it up

for a general debrief, "Which dynamic most grabbed your attention? Why? How does that manifest itself in your organization? Specific strategies to compensate?"

## SEVEN DYNAMICS OF CHANGE DEBRIEF

1. **People will feel awkward, ill at ease and self-conscious.** How many of you felt uncomfortable, awkward, ill at ease and self-conscious during this exercise? Do you think employees feel this during change in our organization? The key is to acknowledge these reactions without making employees feel guilty. When introducing change, perhaps we could simply say, "Folks, I understand you will feel uncomfortable and ill-at-ease during the next few months. That's understandable. I will be feeling the same way..."

2. **People initially focus on what they have to give up versus what they have to gain.** The directions were "Change three things" not "Take three things off." But we naturally start taking things off. Like great salespeople, we should be selling features and benefits during change. Even for positive changes, we tend to focus on what we'll be losing. Consider this approach, "I understand your concern regarding learning a new billing system, but the payoff will be less weekend shifts and more time with your family!" Again, features and benefits.

3. **People will feel alone even if everyone else is going through the same change.** How many felt as if you were the only crazy people taking clothes off during that exercise? How many feel you're the only person/department having to implement changes in your organization? Simply getting your people together and allowing them to share their reactions to a given change can be beneficial. Avoid letting this turn into a gripe session. Be creative and consider sub-grouping having each group report back the most difficult challenges with the proposed change and specific strategies to ensure a smooth implementation.

4. **People can handle only so much change.** An elephant can be eaten one bite at a time. With three changes, most participants were fine. When five more changes were added, most started to feel very uncomfortable. Five more, 13 total, a riot became a real possibility!

I conducted this exercise with a university board of directors when the president told the following story. He had just arrived on campus and was excited about what he saw as opportunities to take the university to the next level. He went home and listed 125 things he wanted to address. The good news is that he wrote them down. The bad news is that he shared the list! His staff was overwhelmed. He admitted that a better approach would have been to categorize that list into three categories (students, faculty, and buildings) instead of sharing all 125 items. The key is to prioritize change and not overwhelm your employees.

5. **People are at different levels of readiness for change**.

   I love change. If someone were to call and say, "Greg, we love your home and want to purchase it. The only thing is that we need you out next week." I would feel a little pinched for time but my general philosophy is, "Adapt & Deal." My wife, on the other hand, needs more time to process change than me. Not that one is right and the other wrong, just different levels of readiness for change. During the change exercise, a few were uncomfortable even with just three changes while some were asking for more changes even at the end of the exercise. The key is to understand and appreciate how your employees react to change and as much as possible, customize your approach as needed. Most importantly, avoid making others feel guilty for their reaction to change.

6. **People will be concerned they don't have enough resources.** The instructions were, "Change three things in your personal appearance," not, "Take three things off." During most exercises, there will be numerous items on the table (pencils, paper, phones, etc.) that can easily be placed in pockets, pants, meeting the required changes. Back at the

workplace, how often do we limit our options based on the perceived notion that we don't have enough resources (time, money, people, etc.)? The key is to challenge our teams to think "outside the nine dots."

The following exercise is a powerful example of how we limit our creativity based on an unconscious need to stay within self-imposed boundaries.

## THINKING OUTSIDE THE 9 DOTS EXERCISE
### Directions

Place nine dots on a flip chart (see Figure 1) and ask participants to:

- Connect all nine dots using just four straight lines
- Without lifting your pen or pencil
- Without re-tracing any of the lines

Give participants a few minutes to work. If participants cannot Figure it out after a few minutes, complete the exercise for them (see Figure 2).

Debrief: How does this apply to your organization? Challenges? Key points:

- We often limit our creativity by trying to "stay in the lines."
- Creativity and innovation often occur "outside the lines."

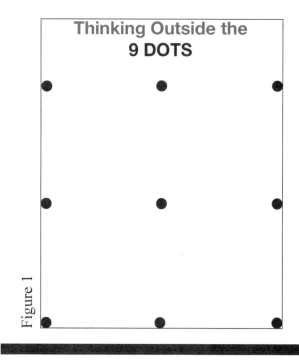

Figure 1

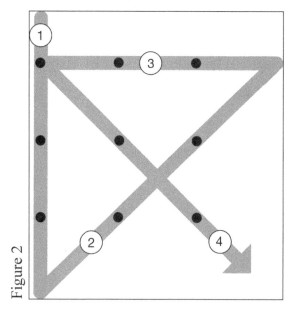

Figure 2

- There are times when staying "within the lines" is appropriate (rules, laws, regulations, compliance, safety).
- Breakthroughs often occur "outside the lines."

7. **If you take the pressure off, people revert back to their old behavior.** Yes, people go back to old ways even if the change is more comfortable! During this exercise it's not uncommon for people to remove shoes, ties, belts, etc. But as soon as the exercise is over, the more restricted clothing goes back on! Even if it was more comfortable with our changes, we tend to revert back to our old ways.

As a workshop leader, I'm still partial to flip charts and whiteboards. I can remember a previous manager peeking in my classroom and just shaking her head whenever I resisted PowerPoint and reverted back to my trusted flip chart. She kept the pressure on and now I couldn't function without PowerPoint. And that's the key. We have to keep the pressure on lest our employees slip back to the old ways.

*The seven dynamics of change were adapted from an article by Ken Blanchard, and published in The Inside Guide, Oct. 1992.*

## QUESTIONS FOR CONSIDERATION

1. How is change impacting your organization?
2. How do you personally react to change?
3. Why do people resist change?
4. What strategies for being a Change Agent work best? Least?
5. How creative or innovative would you say your organization is?
6. Describe situations where "staying within the lines" is necessary and appropriate? Situations where we should be thinking "outside the lines?"

## CHANGE: IT'S YOUR CALL

Have there been moments in your life when you thought you were right, and didn't see the need to change, only to face a big disaster? There's an old story of a near collision between a large naval ship and what at first appears to be another vessel. It's a classic anecdote, which illustrates the perils of stubbornness and the need to change.

The naval vessel requests that the other ship change course. The other party responds that the naval vessel should change course, whereupon the captain of the naval vessel repeats the demand, identifying himself and the ship he commands, and making threats. The following is a transcript of that encounter.

Naval Ship: "Please divert your course 15 degrees to the North to avoid a collision."

Other Party: "Recommend you divert YOUR course 15 degrees to the South to avoid a collision."

Naval Ship: "This is the captain of a US Navy ship. I say again, divert YOUR course."

Other Party: "No, I say again, you divert YOUR course."

Naval Ship: "This is the Aircraft Carrier USS Abraham Lincoln, the second largest ship in the United States' Atlantic fleet. Three Destroyers, three Cruisers and numerous support vessels accompany us. I demand that YOU change your course 15 degrees North! That's One-Five degrees North or counter measures will be undertaken to ensure the safety of this ship and my crew!"

Other Party: "This is a lighthouse. Your call."

# Chapter 19

## Steps of Team Growth

Bruce W. Tuckman devised the stages of team growth in 1965. Its basic premise is that teams go through predictable stages of growth: Form, Storm, Norm, and Perform (Figure 1). It is a fluid process with

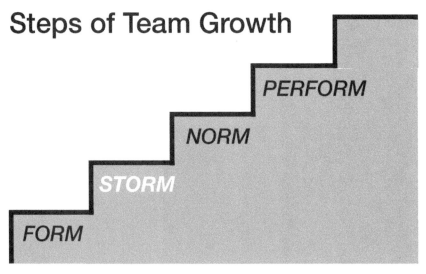

Figure 1

the team automatically going back to the Form stage whenever there's a change in membership (someone comes in, someone leaves).

Because of this phenomenon, most teams are understandably and regrettably in constant flux. Even when team membership is constant, most teams are stuck in a "Storming" stage due to the natural avoidance of conflict and hoping it will somehow fix itself or simply go away. Unfortunately, it rarely does either (fix itself or go away). While most teams lack a systematic process for dealing with conflict, the irony of the Storm stage is a team will never get to the Norm and Perform stage without going through the Storm stage.

The following are both characteristics and suggested actions needed for each stage of Team Growth:

**Stage 1: Form**

The focus of the Form stage is to determine how one fits in and who's in control. Most team members are polite, often sitting back evaluating the situation, and reluctant to be the first one to speak up. What's needed in the Form stage but rarely occurs is a formal orientation, particularly when a new member joins the team. The Form stage is a perfect opportunity for a leader to assemble the entire team for introductions. Additionally, this orientation serves as an opportunity to review mission, vision, key goals and objectives. It might sound something like this:

"Team, I would like to welcome Greg and introduce him to our team. As many know, Greg has an extensive background in training and development and will be heading up our new leadership development organization. He will be talking with everyone, and creating some plans later this year as we build this new division of our company. I'm going to let Greg tell you more about himself, his role and expectations of how we can support him. After that, I would like each of you to go around the room and introduce yourself, tell Greg about your role in our organization and your expectations of how he can support your efforts. After everyone is introduced, we will review our mission, vision, key goals and objectives. Greg, again welcome and let's go ahead and get started."

Unfortunately, here's what usually happens: "Greg, welcome! I've got to be out of town for the rest of the week. I'm sorry; I would love to spend more time with you. We'll try to get together later. In the meantime, if you need something, Pam will be able to assist you. Again, welcome!"

As you can imagine, and perhaps experienced, the proper orientation rarely happens.

A key component of a proper orientation is a review of mission, vision, goals, objectives, key milestones, leadership expectations, etc. In addition to introducing the new team member to these important organizational facts, it is a wonderful review for current team members. While the next stage (Storm) usually cannot be avoided, it can be minimized with a well-designed orientation.

**Stage 2: Storm**

A major reason teams enter the Storm stage is a lack of role clarity, which is even more reason for covering the topic of Roles in the Form stage. Other causes for the Storm stage vary from personality conflicts to resistance to organizational change (no surprise there). Bottom line, there's no avoiding the Storm stage and, as mentioned earlier, your team will never reach the next two stages (Norm/Perform) unless you successfully navigate through the Storm stage.

Unfortunately, most teams attempt to avoid this stage, and turn a blind eye to the valid reasons for addressing this stage head on. The keys are the courage to acknowledge you and your teams are in the Storm stage, a willingness to address the reasons for being stuck in Storm, a commitment to explore strategies for getting out of this stage, and the vision to ultimately reach the Perform stage. It is important to note that most teams go in and out of the Storm stage several times throughout the organizational life cycle.

In my consulting business, I assist teams with "Storming Sessions." These sessions must not turn into a "gripe sessions." Issues, not people, should be attacked with clearly stated and adhered to guidelines. I suggest a trained facilitator to direct these sessions so it doesn't get out of hand create more "storm" than even before.

## Stage 3: Norm

When a team successfully navigates the Storm stage, the Norm stage is just around the corner. The Norm stage is where the group starts to work together as a team. Competition begins to give way to cooperation. Differences are resolved and diversity of opinion appreciated. The team is starting to click. In the Form and Storm stages, management is more appropriate. In the Norm and Perform stages, leadership is best suited.

Using the Situational Leadership/Management model, which we will explore in the next chapter, a Directive Style is the most appropriate in the Form stage, with Coaching in the Storm stage, Supportive in the Norm stage, and Delegation in the Perform stage.
Stage 4: Perform

Peak performance and organizational excellence are hallmarks of the Perform stage.
Key Point: Whenever there is a change of team membership (someone joins, someone leaves), the team automatically goes back to the Form stage.

QUESTIONS FOR CONSIDERATION

1. What stage of team growth would you say your immediate team is in? Explain.

2. How can your team transition to the next stage?

3. How good of a job does your organization do with orientation in the Form stage? Explain.

4. What are the reasons for a team regressing to a previous stage?

5. Why is the Storm stage difficult for teams and their organizations?

6. What specific strategies would you suggest for navigating through the Storm stage?

7. Describe a time when your team went through all four stages.

*Psychologist Bruce Tuckman first came up with the memorable phrase "forming, storming, norming, and performing" in his 1965 article, "Developmental Sequence in Small Groups," He used it to describe the path that most teams follow on their way to high performance.*

# Chapter 20

## Leadership

Management consultants Paul Hersey and Ken Blanchard first introduced the situational leadership/management model in the late 60s. As with the Social Styles model described in Chapter 12, the challenge is the same.

> *"If you're favorite tool is a hammer,*
> *be careful not to treat everyone else like a nail."*

Translation: one's management and leadership should be based on the needs of the follower versus the leaders most preferred style. Unfortunately, we often manage and lead based on our most preferred style and how we have been managed and led. The result is we're either under- or over–managing and leading others.

Historically, we've gone from a predominately management focus, which originated during the Industrial Revolution to a predominately leadership focus. From the Industrial Revolution up until the 1980s, it was about managing people. Manufacturing became highly automated process with emphasis on production and compliance. Both my parents were factory workers and never expected or received much satisfaction from their work. It was an "end justifies the means" mentality. For the most part, my parents' jobs were routine and they didn't have to think that much on the job. The machine did the job and they simply managed the machine. It was the means to support their family.

In the late 70s and early 80s, the focus started to switch from manufacturing to a service economy. Jobs required employee involvement and input. From compliance to commitment, leadership became its own discipline. Concepts like empowerment, self-direction, vision, and inspiration—and "Soft Skills" gained credibility and popularity.

Management gurus like Warren Bennis made statements like, "Most organizations are over managed and under led." Younger generations saw how their parents had been managed with little job satisfaction, and naturally started choosing leading over managing. Buts it's not, "Leadership versus Management" or even "Leadership or Management." It's "Leadership and Management." There are times to manage and there are times to lead.

Naturally, for most of us leadership is more enjoyable, which explains the numerous phone calls I receive about personnel issues in my coaching business. Those conversations go something like this, "Greg, I have this real jerk for a direct report. He talks down to everyone, he won't take my feedback, and I've given him plenty of chances to improve. I'm at my wit's end and don't know what to do." My response is usually something like this, "Fire him!" In this situation, management, not leadership, is needed and apparently long overdue.

Metaphorically speaking, when you were hired you raised your right hand and took an oath.

## THE OATH

I agree that I will lead in addition to manage.

I agree that I will lead in addition to follow.

I agree that I will conduct in addition to facilitate.

I agree that I will Drive in addition to Ride.

I agree that I will develop my Hard Skills in addition to my
   Soft Skills.

I agree that I will strive for credibility in addition to likeability.

I agree that I will lead from the brain in addition from the heart.

I agree that I will see the scaffold in addition to the cathedral.

I agree that I will be mission-driven in addition to vision-focused.

I agree that I will be tactical in addition to strategic.

I agree that I will listen in addition to talk.

I agree that I will be task-focused in addition to relationship-focused.

# Chapter 21

## The Situational Leadership/Management Model

The Situational Leadership/Management Model is a wonderful tool to balance both sides of the equation: management and leadership.

Direct your attention to the horizontal axis in Figure 1 – this is the task that needs to be accomplished. Then take a look at the vertical axis – this is the relationship that must be developed to accomplish the task.

At the top left is High, bottom left Low and bottom right High. (High Relationship, Low Relationship. High Task, Low Task). "High" doesn't mean "all" and "Low" doesn't mean "none." High Task, Low Relationship simply means the focus is more on the Task versus the Relationship.

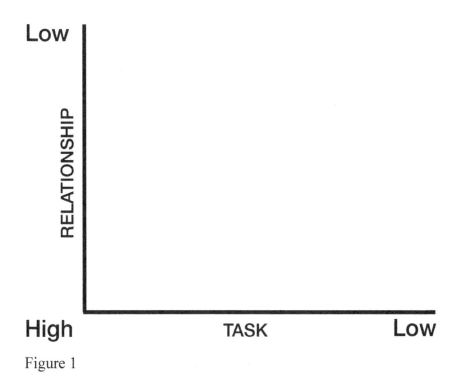

Figure 1

Complete the model in Figure 2 and you have the Situational/ Management Model. The bell-shaped curve implies that a manager/ leader over time should move a direct report from having to manage them (quadrant one) to leading them (quadrant four). As a direct report, this should also be a goal (from being managed to being led) as one gains both skills and confidence.

The first quadrant is High Task and Low Relationship. High doesn't mean all and Low doesn't mean none. This style is called Directive and is characterized by one-way communication focusing

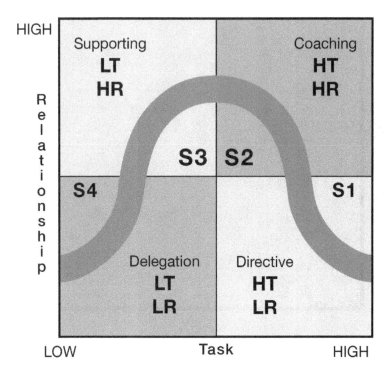

HIGH

R e l a t i o n s h i p

Supporting
**LT
HR**

Coaching
**HT
HR**

**S3** | **S2**

**S4**

**S1**

Delegation
**LT
LR**

Directive
**HT
LR**

LOW          **Task**          HIGH

Figure 2

on the task at hand. My son Will worked at a manufacturing plant in college. His boss Dave clearly modeled Situational Leadership/ Management. The following is an example of the evolution from managing Will to leading him:

Dave: "Will, welcome, glad you're here. I want to tell you our mission, our expectations, your role, etc. After that briefing, Dave continues: Now let's go see Cliff who's our director of engineering. I'll introduce you and he'll give you a briefing on your internship. You'll be with him for the first month or so. Good luck, again glad you're here. [High Task, Low Relationship. Will's a new employee; this was exactly what he needed.]

The second quadrant is High Task, High Relationship and is called Coaching. Characterized by two-way communication, Coaching provides an opportunity for give and take, and questions. In this example, Will's been on the job several months now when Dave meets with him:

"Will, good to see you again. I hear good things about you. Here's what I want you to do next. I want to prepare you to give tours of our plant. As you know, thousands of people visit our plant each year, and the tours are a great PR tool for our business. I have confidence in you and after a month or so you'll be giving at least two tours each day. You'll have time to learn and practice the script and shadow our current tour guides. Any questions, Will?"

Will asks, "Will I be able to go back to engineering at some point?" Great question, Dave exclaims! "Yes, eventually, but I would like for you to be exposed to different departments. So for the next month or so, you'll be in Human Resources with Wendy as you prepare for your tour duties. Other questions, Will?"

The third quadrant, Supporting, is High Relationship, Low Task. Will's been on the job now over one year and Dave calls him into his office:

"Will, we've got an issue. Seems we've been getting less than favorable feedback on our tours. I'm not sure what the issue is but you're one of our best and I have confidence you'll be able to get to the bottom of this. Gather your data and let's get back together to brainstorm possible solutions in a few weeks." Will may respond, "Dave, are you sure you want me to tackle this? I'm just an intern." Dave responds, "Will, you can do this. I have all the faith in the world in you. See you in a few weeks, and let me know if you have any questions."

Hopefully, you're seeing the progression from "Management" to increasing emphasis on "Leadership." Dave wouldn't have given Will that last assignment had Will only been there a few months, any more than he would treat Will like a new employee after he's been there over a year. Again, if you're favorite tool is a hammer, be careful not to treat everyone else like a nail.

The fourth quadrant, Delegation, is Low Task, Low Relationship. And as my late father used to say, "Don't stand in between the dog and the tree." Will's been on the job now for almost three years and he doesn't see Dave that often. Will knows his job, does his job and doesn't need much direction. Will meets with Dave once a quarter for a general update. Delegation doesn't mean abdication. It's just not hands-on and less frequent.

## WHICH STYLE TO USE AND WHEN

Because the Situation Leadership/Management model is follower-driven, the most appropriate Style to use is dependent upon the Readiness Level of the employee being managed/led for a particular task (see Figure 3). The key words in the previous sentience being "for a particular task." People don't have readiness levels, tasks do. This is important because we tend to label others based on their overall skills versus their ability to perform a particular task, which leads to either over and/or under managing and leading.

For example, let's say your organization hires me as the director of training and development. Appropriately, my manager pretty much lets me run that department because he understands and recognizes my 20-plus years of experience. So I get labeled as a "Readiness Level 4" employee, which as I mentioned earlier doesn't exist (people don't have readiness levels, tasks do).

Let's say another part of my job responsibility is quarterly presentations to senior management on the company's financials. Because of the complexity of the numbers, mastery of excel spreadsheets is a necessity. The problem is I'm not overly technical and avoid excel and other technical applications. Because my boss has labeled me as a "Readiness Level 4 employee," she is surprised and embarrassed during the meeting when she sees that I've ditched the PowerPoint and superimposed the company financials on a flip chart!

## READINESS LEVELS
"People don't have Readiness Level; Tasks do."

**RI:** Low Skills and/or Understanding
Low Desire and/or Confidence

*Discussion:* Notice the and/or in each level. A new employee may have high skills but low understanding of the industry. He/she may have high desire to start working but lack the confidence to jump right in. Management; not leadership is needed.

**R2:** Low Skills and/or Understanding
High Desire and Confidence

*Discussion:* An employee may still lack understanding but is highly motivated. The key is to restrain without squelching enthusiasm. Management; not leadership is needed.

**R3**: High Skills and Understanding
Low Desire and/or Confidence

*Discussion:* This could be a burnout situation or someone who has lost their edge. They need leadership more than management. They need a pat on the back, encouragement. They lack desire and/or confidence, not skills/understanding.

**R4:** High Skills and Understanding
High Desire and Confidence

*Discussion:* Get out of the way. Don't smother. Appreciate their efforts. Stay in touch. Delegation does not mean abdication. Periodic follow-up is important.

Figure 3

In this example, I would be a Readiness Level 1 for this particular task but my boss under managed by Delegating an important job to an unprepared employee.

Organizations should train all employees on the Situational Leadership/Management Model with particular focus on Readiness Levels. In partnership with one's immediate manager, an employee lists individual goals and objectives, agreeing on readiness levels for each. After coming to a consensus on each goal and objective and readiness level, it shouldn't be a surprise when certain tasks dictate more hands-on management (Directive/Coaching) while others take less hands-on management (Supportive/Delegation).

# Matching Readiness Level to Style

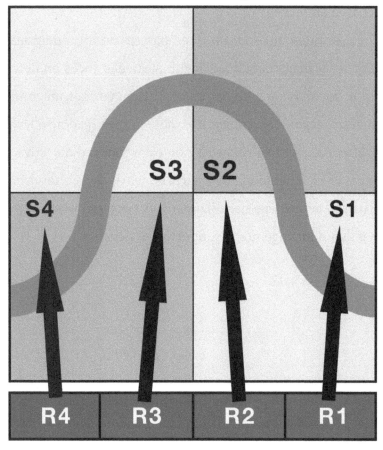

QUESTIONS FOR CONSIDERATION

1. Why do managers and leaders find themselves operating out of only one or two styles?

2. What is the impact of operating out of only one or two styles?

3. How do we label employees and what is the danger of doing so?

4. Discuss the differences between management and leadership in your organization.

5. Which one is easiest for you and why?

6. Which is most important in your organization and why?

7. Why are Readiness Levels important?

# Chapter 22

## The 12 Elements of Great Managing

More than a decade ago, Gallup took a broad assessment of how organizations were managing their people and determined that most organizations were "shooting in the dark." Gallup concluded the typical organization would commission an excruciating long employee opinion survey, hoping that somewhere among 100-200 questions it would stumble upon the most important concepts. When the numbers were crunched, they were very often too confusing to understand or form the basis for reliable observations.

Even more alarming, top management assumed there was a general level of "satisfaction" that pretty much applied throughout the organization, and that they (the senior team) were the main drivers of their employees' feelings. All these assumptions were wrong.

Gallup examined the one million employee interviews then in its database, the hundreds of questions that had been asked over the preceding decades, and every variable on business-unit performance that organizations had supplied with their employee rosters. These data were analyzed to find which survey questions—and therefore which aspects of work—were most powerful in explaining workers' productive motivations on the job.

Ultimately, 12 elements of great managing (and work life) emerged from the research as the core of the unwritten social contract between employee and employer. Through their answers to the dozen most important questions and their daily actions that affected performance, the million workers were saying, *"If you do these things for us, we will do what the organization needs of us."*

[How would you answer the following as an employee? How would your employees answer the following questions, which is valuable feedback for you as their manager?]

1. I know what is expected of me at work.
2. I have the materials and equipment I need to do my work.
3. At work, I have the opportunity to do what I do best every day.
4. In the last seven days, I have received recognition or praise for doing good work.
5. My supervisor seems to care about me as a person.
6. There is someone at work who encourages my development.
7. At work, my opinion seems to count.

8. The mission or purpose of my organization makes me feel my job is important.

9. My associates or fellow employees are committed to doing quality work.

10. I have a best friend at work.

11. In the last six months, someone at work has talked to me about my progress.

12. This last year, I have had opportunities at work to learn and grow.

Source: *The Elements of Great Managing* by James K. Harter & Rod Wagner, Gallup Press 2006.

# Chapter 23

## The Five Practices of Exemplary Leadership

In their study, Jim Kouzes and Barry Posner set out to discover what it took to become a great leader. They wanted to know the common practices of ordinary men and women when they were at their leadership best—when they were able to take people to levels of achievement they had never been before. Their analysis of thousands of cases and surveys revealed The Five Practices of Exemplary Leadership.

### MODEL THE WAY

Leaders establish principles concerning the way people (constituents, peers, colleagues, and customers alike) should be treated and the way goals should be pursued. They create standards of excellence and then set an example for others to follow. Because the prospect of complex change can overwhelm people and stifle action, they set interim goals so that people can achieve small wins as they work toward larger objectives. They unravel bureaucracy when it impedes action; they put up signposts when people are unsure of where to go or how to get there; and they create opportunities for victory.

## INSPIRE A SHARED VISION

Leaders passionately believe that they can make a difference. They envision the future, creating an ideal and unique image of what the organization can become. Through their magnetism and quiet persuasion, leaders enlist others in their dreams. They breathe life into their visions and get people to see exciting possibilities for the future.

## CHALLENGE THE PROCESS

Leaders search for opportunities to change the status quo. They look for innovative ways to improve the organization. In doing so, they experiment and take risks. And because leaders know that risk taking involves mistakes and failures, they accept the inevitable disappointments as learning opportunities.

## ENABLE OTHERS TO ACT

Leaders foster collaboration and build spirited teams. They actively involve others. Leaders understand that mutual respect is what sustains extraordinary efforts; they strive to create an atmosphere of trust and human dignity. They strengthen others, making each person feel capable and powerful.

## ENCOURAGE THE HEART

Accomplishing extraordinary things in organizations is hard work. To keep hope and determination alive, leaders recognize contributions that individuals make. In every winning team, the members need to share in the rewards of their efforts, so leaders celebrate accomplishments. They make people feel like heroes.

## QUESTIONS FOR CONSIDERATION

1. How would you rate yourself on each practice of exemplary leadership?
2. Which one(s) would you consider to be your strengths? Weakness?
3. Which one(s) would you consider to be your organization's strengths? Weakness? (your leadership team in general)

Source: *The Five Practices of Exemplary Leadership* by Barry Posner & James Kouzes, John Wiley & Sons, Inc., 2012.

# Chapter 24

## Be-Know-Do

I first heard of General Carmen Cavezza (U.S. Army Ret.) from a friend of mine in Columbus, Georgia. Like General Dan Cherry, General Cavezza continues to lead and inspire others when most folks who have achieved what they have are slowing down. General Cavezza retired from the United States Army where he was the Base Commander at Fort Benning, the nation's largest army base. My friend had just heard the retired general speak to a group of business people and quickly emailed me a summary of his "Soft Skill" points:

- Never depend on the first report, especially if it's an emotional issue.
- Be yourself—the best leader you can be is you.
- Establish and live your values.

- If you have good people, get out of their way and let them be good.
- Look for the pony in the barn and not just the poop on the floor.
- Be an optimist.
- Be a good listener—James 1:19 says, "Be swift to hear, slow to speak, slow to wrath."
- Be patient—what looks bad at the end of the day will look better the next morning.
- Don't accept problems from people without hearing their suggested solution.
- Always strive to be better—when you die, there's always unused space in our brains.
- When you're satisfied, you're ineffective.

I couldn't wait to meet General Cavezza and as I waited in the conference room, I anticipated his perspective on leadership. Would he reference Peter Drucker or would he cite the military leadership of Generals Patton, Schwarzkopf, or Powell? Would he be a Blanchard or a Covey follower? General Cavezza was indeed an impressive man, yet his presence and his character made me feel comfortable and at ease. His response, simple yet powerful, was very much like his demeanor. "Greg, I can sum up my general perspective on leadership in three simple words: Be-Know-Do."

Wondering what leadership book he must have read, and one that I had obviously overlooked in my two decades of studying the subject, I asked, "Be-Know-Do?"

His response, "Be-Know-Do, it's in the Army Leadership Field Manual 22-100, which lays out the framework that applies to all Army leaders—officer and NCO, military and civilian, active and reserve. At the core of our leadership doctrine are the same Army values embedded in our force: Loyalty, Duty, Respect, Selfless Service, Honor, Integrity, and Personal Courage."

General Cavezza continued, "The Army does two things everyday: It trains soldiers and develops leaders. When leadership in business breaks down, employees become disengaged, the culture deteriorates, and profits can spiral out of control. When leadership in our Armed Forces breaks down, people die." Leadership in business is important; leadership in the Army is essential!

General Cavezza defined leadership as influencing people by providing purpose, direction, and motivation while operating to accomplish the mission and improving the organization. "In short, leadership in the Army transforms human potential into effective performance," according to Cavezza.

That small conference room was quickly transformed into a classroom as the professor continued the lecture that would change my entire perspective on leadership. General Cavezza said that we demonstrate character through our behavior and one of the key responsibilities of a leader is to teach values to subordinates. Therefore, the General explained, Army leadership begins with what the leader must BE, with the values and attributes that shape a leader's character.

He described the Army values as:

- *Loyalty*: Bearing true faith and allegiance to the U.S. Constitution, the Army, the unit, and other soldiers.

- *Duty*: Fulfilling all obligations.

- *Respect*: Treating people as they should be treated.

- *Selfless service*: Putting the welfare of the nation, the Army, and subordinates before one's own.

- *Honor*: Living up to all the Army values.

- *Integrity*: Doing what's right—legally and morally.

- *Personal courage*: Facing fear, danger, or adversity (physical or moral.)

Skills are those things people KNOW how to do, such as competence from the technical side of a job and the people skills required for leadership. Leaders must have a high level of knowledge and mastery of four basic skills:

- *Interpersonal Skills*: coaching, teaching, counseling, motivating and empowering others, as well as building teams.

- *Conceptual Skills*: The ability to think creatively and to reason analytically, critically, and ethically which is the basis of sound judgment.
- *Technical skills*: Job-related abilities that is necessary to accomplish the task at hand.
- *Tactical skills*: In the Army, those skills required to deploy units into combat.

And while character and knowledge are necessary, leaders must apply what they know; they must act and DO what they have learned is effective. Successful leaders build teams, execute plans, and lead change in their organizations. In the Army's language, the three areas that a leader must DO are:

- *Influence*: Using Interpersonal Skills to lead others toward a goal, Communicating Clearly, Motivating Others and Recognizing Achievement.
- *Operate*: Developing and Executing Plans, Managing Resources, Identifying Strengths and Weaknesses.
- *Improve*: Good leaders strive to leave the organization in better shape than they found it. They believe in Life-Long Learning, always seeking Self-Improvement, and Organization Growth and Development. Good leaders are also Change Agents.

At the end of my time with General Cavezza, I was speechless. I have attended hundreds of seminars, listened to hours and hours of lectures, read a room full of books and yet never thought of spending time with the epitome of a leader: a Military Officer. And sadly since the end of the draft and the establishment of the all-volunteer force in 1973, fewer and fewer civilians are being exposed to the Army, its leadership and its training. And ironically, many of us live only a short distance from a military base where numerous opportunities to learn from the nation's most committed team of soldiers and the most effective leaders in the world wait for us to simply call the public information officer and arrange a tour and a briefing from the Base Commander and his leadership team.

## QUESTIONS FOR CONSIDERATION

1. What are your general thoughts about military leadership?
2. What are your thoughts about the perceived "tough love" leadership approach in the military?
3. How do you think military leadership has evolved over the years?
4. What are the major challenges of military leadership today?
5. What can we learn from military leadership?
6. How can civilian leadership capitalize on military leadership? (Would you consider visiting a local military base?)
7. What are the similarities between civilian leadership and military leadership?

8. What could the military learn from the private sector?

9. How does "Be-Know-Do" relate to "Soft Skills?" Which ones are "Soft" and which ones are "Hard/Technical?"

## DEALERS OF HOPE

Rosey Grier, a member of the "Fearsome Foursome," when he played with the Los Angeles Rams and now a Christian minister and inspirational speaker relays a powerful message he delivered when working with inner-city youth in Los Angeles. Rosey said, "Leaders aren't dealers of dope, they're dealers of hope!" As leaders, we must be "Dealers of Hope."

## THE AMAZING POWER AND RESPONSIBILITY OF LEADERSHIP

When the people you supervise go home for the day, whom do you think they're talking about over the dinner table? Most likely, it's not the CEO of your company. It's probably not even a senior manager within your company. If you have direct reports, they're talking about you more than you probably realize. How you treat them impacts them not only at work, but influences their entire life! What an amazing responsibility power and responsibility we have with the people with whom we work.

And it goes much further than simply a direct report's immediate family. I was having dinner with a friend and asked about his older brother. My friend responded, "We're really worried about Steve. His boss is horrible and it's literally killing him." Wow! So, this one toxic manager is negatively impacting a direct report, his spouse and children, his brother and many others who are concerned and worried about his situation. Never ever underestimate the amazing power and responsibility of being a leader. Leadership is not an option! Manage the business, but lead your people.

## QUESTIONS FOR CONSIDERATION

1. What are your direct reports saying about you over the dinner table?

2. As a leader, are you a source of motivation or a source of stress?

## BOSS VERSUS LEADER

| BOSS VS. LEADER | |
|---|---|
| **BOSS** | **LEADER** |
| Directs | Coaches |
| Relies on Authority | Relies on Goodwill/Trust |
| Issues Ultimatums | Generates Enthusiasm |
| "I" | "We" |
| Utilizes Human Resources | Develops People |
| Takes Credit | Gives Credit |
| Places the Blame | Accepts Blame |
| "Go" | "Let's Go!" |
| My Way | Strength in Unity |
| Compliance | Commitment |
| Conducts | Facilitates |

*"If you know, you can manage. If you love, you can lead!"*

*Greg Coker*

# Chapter 25

## Culture

## CULTURE — THE PERSONALITY
## OF YOUR ORGANIZATION

I can get a good feel of the culture of an organization after only a few minutes of walking in the front door. How I'm greeted, the cleanliness of the office, company vehicles and uniforms, the smell, how employees interact with each other, the artwork, the hierarchical structure of the parking lot, all speak volumes about the culture of that organization. Culture, or the personality of an organization, is a system of shared assumptions (often unwritten), values, and beliefs, which governs how people behave and interact within an organization.

From how employees dress (formal culture like a bank to a more casual dress code at an engineering firm) to where they park (reserved parking for the "big dogs" speaks, or barks, loudly on who the organization values most). School Systems have a definable culture. As a high school student, I remember our school's high performance culture of both academics and sports. Our principal was a former coach and balanced leader who ran a tight ship but in a loving and respectful manner. 30 years later, I was a member of the school board having a different view of school culture witnessing first-hand the role of leadership as "Keeper of the Culture."

## THE ROLE OF A LEADER IN SHAPING CULTURE

While on the school board and after numerous principals who ran a tight ship, an elementary school principal took the helm at our high school. While he was effective with seven to ten year olds, he lost control with teenagers. The culture quickly went from a tight run ship to a rudderless organization where student discipline was lacking and performance quickly slipping.

Using the "Bus" metaphor from Chapter 9, he should have been on the "Bus" but he was clearly in the "Wrong Seat." The high school culture was spiraling out of control.

His warm demeanor and congenial disposition, absent a firm disciplinarian and an "in control" presence, was a recipe for disaster. We found a more appropriate seat for him and started a search for a "Fit" versus the previous "Fix." During the interim, we hired a retired high school principal with a firm, no nonsense reputation to complete the semester until we could hire a permanent replacement.

In our haste, we hired someone more suited to run a high security prison than a high school. We learned a valuable lesson and struck a balance of discipline and compassion with a permanent principal. He not only created a winning culture, he was later awarded the state's principal of the year! The private sector could learn from school systems on the amount of time and analysis dedicated in finding the most appropriate leader.

## MANAGEMENT & LEADERSHIP; OPERATIONAL RESULTS & CULTURE

After 20 plus years in corporate America and having taken a sabbatical in public service (Utility Regulator), I returned to the private sector as a division officer for a large utility. I was recruited by and reported to our state president who was the definition of culture. He was visible with employees, active in the community and believed in developing relationships with local and state leaders. He preached of being "intentional" in our leadership and living the company values 24/7. We worked hard and we played hard. While the culture thrived, the bottom line suffered.

A larger division within our company needed a "Culture" guy as their relationships with local and state leaders were suffering. Employees weren't engaged and the company's spirit needed re-ignited. Our division president was promoted and replaced with a

"Financial" guy. Unfortunately, our new leader's personality (or lack thereof), lack of Soft Skills and general indifference to culture quickly destroyed what his processor had built.

In retrospect, what was missing, should have been expected and demanded by senior management was a balance between culture and performance. One division president was clearly more leadership and culture focused while the latter more management and operational focused. While Warren Bennis is widely quoted as saying most organizations are over managed and under led, I think he would agree a balance of the two would be ideal.

## DEFINING & LEADING YOUR CULTURE

Defining and leading your culture starts at the top. I was retained by a university vice president for facilities management responsible for over 300 grounds keepers, custodians, and physical plant employees. New in this position, he sincerely believed his organization was the most important department in the entire university system as they interfaced with faculty, staff and students every day.

He heard my "Building Cathedrals: The Power of Purpose" speech and envisioned a culture of "Cathedral Builders" versus "Bricklayers." He invited me to present my speech, followed by his passionate presentation to employees, where he outlined culture, value, expectations and appreciation for a job well done.

## TO OVERWHELM THE OLD CULTURE,
## A LEADER MUST MOVE QUICKLY AND
## ACHIEVE CRITICAL MASS

While logistically challenging, the university vice president managed to get all employees in one location where he outlined what the culture was going to be under his leadership. Delivered in a passionate and motivating fashion, he demonstrated his appreciation for hard work and helped everyone see the "Cathedral." He did this within the first six months of taking the helm of this organization.

His speech was infused with colorful metaphors (Cathedrals), testimonials from students who had been personally touched by facilities management employees and numerous stories of Extraordinary Customer Service. Metaphors, Testimonies and Stories are key ingredients of defining, building and maintaining organizational culture.

## SPEED OF THE TEAM; SPEED OF THE LEADER

I give fast food restaurants a hard time, as they are often not the best examples of customer service, especially when I'm in a hurry and choose the Drive Thru versus dining inside. In the upcoming Customer Service chapter, I introduce the "What Customers Want" model. Listed at the top is "Friendly Service." After the pre-recorded "friendly voice," what usually follows is a curt, "Order when you're ready!" screech.

However, on occasion I receive a friendly voice welcoming me with a, "Good morning!! What can I get for you," followed by, "Please drive to the second window for your breakfast." Inevitably, when I drive forward and see the manager, her/his demeanor mirrors the person who took my order. In most cases, if the person at the Drive Thru is rude, the manager has a "No" face if greeted by a friendly and warm employee, the manager appears to have a "Yes" face. As discussed in the Emotional Intelligence chapter, our emotions are contagious. Bottom line, the leader of an organization sets the tone not only for culture, but also for customer service, employee engagement and much more!

## YOU HAVE TO UNDERSTAND THE CULTURE BEFORE YOU CHANGE IT

I was new to a training and development position with a telecommunications company. Excited about implementing the latest tools on empowerment, total quality, team effectiveness, I outlined to my manager, a former no nonsense telephone operator, all the innovative measures I proposed implementing. She let me go on for several minutes and after she had enough gave me probably the best advice I've ever received. "You have to understand the culture before you can change it!"

Take the first six months to listen, observe and ask questions. Practice MBWA, management by walking around. Review company documents, visit employee groups, talk to customers and key stakeholders. Consider a survey and/or questionnaire asking employees to describe how they view the culture of the organization. This time will be well spent in building your credibility and ensuring success during the future cultural transformation.

## SUB-CULTURES

Cultures have Sub-Cultures. In a school system, a High School could have a different culture from the Middle School. Division Head Quarters could have a stuffy corporate feel while a remote Work Center could have a family culture. Such was the case when I worked for the earlier mentioned utility. I was assigned to the stuffy Division Head Quarters with a goal of "lightening things up." It was indeed a tough assignment as that culture was built over a 50-year time frame before our company had acquired it.

Our company made the mistake of assuming that once the purchase was complete the two cultures would naturally merge. The previous company was a very formal company while the acquirer was a more rural informal culture. When I arrived, artwork from the previous company hung in the boardroom, retired officers and board members photos lined the hallway and the "corporate speak" often referred to the old company by name. In short, that old company had never been "put to rest."

Terry Deal, author of Corporate Cultures, described a funeral ritual for companies that had merged. He described actual mourning of the old companies, stories of what made them great with the conclusion being putting to rest that company and associated culture(s). After the funeral ritual, the CEO introduced the new company outlining mission, vision, goals, expectations, etc. Closure and a rebirth achieved!

## BEANS & CORNBREAD CULTURE

Just a few miles down the road from the stuffy Division Head Quarters was a totally different culture. I visited a work center one morning immediately smelling a familiar scent. Standing over an oven was an employee who declared, "Coker, today is beans and cornbread day!" As my eyes lit up having grown up on that country staple, he asked, "You joining us for lunch aren't you?" I responded, "Wouldn't miss it for the world!"

That company's growth strategy included numerous acquisitions creating an obvious challenge of assimilating the acquired companies into a new culture. They secured the services of consulting firm Senn Delaney who developed a program called "Spirit." In addition to culture, the program highlighted many of the Soft Skills outlined in this Field Manual. It was a required workshop for all employees within one's first year of employment attending with their immediate supervisor.

## SUPPORT FOR YOUR ORGANIZATION'S CULTURE

Senn Delaney's Spirit was a hugely successful program, 100 percent supported by top management and integrated within all company initiatives (safety, new employee orientation, etc.). The principles, concepts and values quickly became criteria in the employment process and a benchmark for promotional

**Support for Organizational Culture**

**BEHAVIORS**

| Detractor | Bystander | Advocate |
|---|---|---|

OUTCOMES

| Out the Door | Likely to be Passed by | Opportunities for Advancement |
|---|---|---|

opportunities. In short, this company lived the culture every day. In fact, it was clearly a career-limiting move to be perceived as not living the principles, concepts and values of this program.

## CULTURE AS A RECRUITING TOOL

Recognizing the growing role of culture in attracting and retaining talent, company review and salary comparison website Glassdoor compiled a list of the Top 25 Companies for Culture and Values. According to Glassdoor Career Trends Analyst Scott Dobroski, "Company culture is among the top five factors people consider" when weighing a job offer. And while salary remains firmly installed in spot number one, the importance of company culture in attracting staff is growing. "Company culture is something a lot of great companies are using to lure in great talent, and it's working," says Dobroski.

## QUESTIONS FOR CONSIDERATION

1. How would you define the culture of your organization?
2. Where are the opportunities for improvement?
3. When a new employee joins your organization, what would particularly strike them about your culture?
4. What are the key components of your organizational culture?

5. Which components are motivating? De-motivating?

6. What is the role of the leader in defining and shaping your organizational culture?

7. How good of a job does your organization balance operational results with organizational culture? Which is viewed as more important?

8. Describe the sub-cultures within your organization.

9. How does one demonstrate support for your organization's culture?

10. What are the rewards of actively supporting your organization's culture? Results of not supporting?

11. What are your general thoughts on culture as a competitive advantage in the marketplace? In recruiting new employees? In securing and retaining customers? How much time do you spend discussing culture in the interview process? Is your culture a selling point in the recruiting process?

12. What aspects of culture do you think are enabling regarding innovation and creativity? Which aspects of culture are inhibiting or obstacles to innovation and creativity?

13. What role do metaphors, testimonies and storytelling have in defining, building and maintaining your culture? Describe the metaphors, testimonies and stories that your organization is known.

## SUGGESTIONS FOR ACTIVITIES

Culture Audit/Survey (qualitative and quantitative)

1. Appoint a Culture Team (cross section of employees consisting of new, seasoned, clerical, staff, management, front-line, male, female)

2. Surveying employees, customers and key stakeholders on how they perceive the culture of your organization.

3. Conduct focus group interviews with employees, customers and key stakeholders asking probing questions (How do you perceive the culture of our organization? How could we improve?) regarding the culture of your organization.

4. Interview senior management regarding organizational culture (what it is, importance of, their role in leading, etc.)

5. Review results from the above developing key themes.

6. Present findings to senior management

7.  Present findings to employee body.

8.  Appoint an Implementation Team of a cross section of employees in developing recommendations based on above findings.

9.  Present to senior management

10. Present to employee body

11. Implement approved recommendations

12. Measure results in one year

# Chapter 26

## Customer Service: Back to the Basics

Like most topics we've addressed in Soft Skills Field Manual, we often make it harder than it has to be. Such is the case with Customer Service. A banking client described what he needed from my Customer Service training simply, "Greg, we need to get back to the basics!" The following models are "The Basics" based on Ron Zempkes best-selling book, "Providing Knock Your Socks Off Service."

### WHAT CUSTOMERS REALLY WANT

1. **Friendly Service:** Is it too much to ask that when I walk into a business, a local school, government agency the first person I see is genuinely friendly? Do you have a "Yes" Face or a "No" Face?

Yes Face

That question and the above graphic are based on a powerful story about the third president of the United States, Thomas Jefferson. One day President Jefferson and his entourage were traveling across the country on horseback. They came upon a flooded river with the bridge completely washed away. The decision was made to cross the river on horseback. Rider after rider plunged into the river. About this time, a stranger approached the president and asked if he could ride with him across the river. Without hesitation, the commander-in-chief said, "Yes, hop on!"

After the man slid off the president's horse safely on the other side of the river, the president's modern day secret service scolded him, "Why did you ask the president for a ride across the river? You could have asked any of us." The man explained that he had no idea that he was the president and then said, "Some people have a 'Yes Face,' and some people have a "No" Face. He had a "Yes" Face."

## DO YOU HAVE "NO FACES" IN CUSTOMER INTERFACING ROLES?

Having a Yes Face is no doubt good business, but being able to read other's faces appears to be good business as well. A USA Today article (10-25-11) profiled a hotel that's tailoring their interaction with guests based on body language. Employees have gone through training focusing on what cues to look for in making the customer experience a more pleasant and memorable one. For instance, a customer who makes eye contact while walking down the hall may be more open for conversation. A guest who tugs on his or her ear could indicate stress and be more open to hear about the hotel's yoga kit or a therapeutic pillow.

The key question: Do you have a "Yes" Face that others feel comfortable approaching you? Or do you have a "No" Face that communicates that you're too busy to be interrupted? And sadly, many of the "No" Faces are the ones we put in customer interfacing roles!

Fast food restaurants are notorious for delivering less than friendly service. Pull up to a Drive Thru window and you're likely to hear a voice bark, "Place your order when you're ready!" Realizing the frequency of this problem, many fast food restaurants are using a pre-recorded "Yes" Face (your face is communicated through your voice!) greeting you as you drive up to the window. This rarely works, as the "No" Face at the second window is the lasting experience you remember.

*A man without a smiling face must not open a shop*
*—Chinese Proverb*

2. **Flexibility.** Customers hate rigidity. They understand rules and policies but are not happy when they perceive we're not genuinely considering their request and not an advocate for their needs. There are two types of rules in organizations: *Red Rules* and *Blue Rules.*

*Red Rules* are non-negotiable (laws, regulations, policies). Customers understand Red Rules. We must thoroughly educate the customer regarding a particular rule, regulation, and policy in a respectful, non-demeaning manner (educate; not preach). The message is, "I am very sorry, we're prevented from doing that due to state and federal law," versus, "Nope! Can't do that."

*Blue Rules* are specific to your organization and generally against company policy. Customers get upset when they perceive we're treating *"Blue Rules"* like *"Red Rules."* The message should be, "I'm sorry. I don't think we'll be able to do that. I've never seen it done but here's what I'll do. I will go to my manager and see what I can do. Again, I really don't think I'll have any luck getting this approved, but I will try. Is tomorrow ok for getting back with you?" Bottom line, the customer wants an advocate; not an obstacle.

3. **Problem-Resolution**. When there's a problem, the customer wants it solved! Fix it as quickly as possible, communicate progress with the customer, manage the problem-solving process, communicate with the customer when the problem is solved and most importantly follow-up (in a few days and/or a few weeks) to see if the customer is happy!

4. **Recovery**. I love this one! When we screw up we have the opportunity, if handled appropriately, to make a more loyal customer than before the screw up. The key to that loyalty is in the recovery! Unfortunately, what often happens is when we fail a customer we avoid them at a minimum, and occasionally run from them!

## FOUR STEPS TO RECOVERY

1. **Apology.** The first response is simple, "I'm sorry!" Not, "You don't understand, we had three people call in sick this morning!" The customer doesn't care! Saying sorry will not solve the problem but it will calm an unhappy customer. Sincerity is the key and will occur naturally if we are indeed their advocates.

2. **Urgent Reinstatement.** Our apology will fall flat if we don't address the problem ASAP! Recently, at a local restaurant my dinner was not to my satisfaction. I flagged our waiter

and alerted him of the situation. The first thing out of his mouth was textbook, "I'm sorry. You're a loyal customer and we appreciate you. Again, I'm sorry. Would you like another sandwich or can I get you something else off the menu?" My response, "I'm really craving that bluegrass special." My waiter literally ran to the kitchen. Apology, Urgent Reinstatement.

3. **Symbolic Atonement.** Most customers (some more than others) will expect some type of break/discount once we drop the ball. If possible, some type of "atonement" could be strategic in creating, maintaining and ensuring a satisfied customer. It could be waiving a fee, a free meal (as in the case with my above example) a discount or throwing in an additional service.

4. **Follow-Up.** Customers want to be assured everything is ok. They want to be communicated with. The initial follow-up should be immediate but can also be several days/weeks later as an additional show of concern.

## QUESTIONS FOR CONSIDERATION

1. Why is simple "Friendly Service" such a challenge?
2. How would your customers rate your flexibility?
3. Name "Blue" rules that your organization occasionally treat like "Red" ones. Are your employees aware of the difference?

4. How would you describe/rate your organization's "Problem-Solving?"

5. How would your customer's describe/rate your organization's "Problem-Solving?"

6. How well do you and your organization "Recover?"

7. Which steps of "Recovery" are the most challenging?

8. What are some examples of "Symbolic Atonement" for your organization?

## HUMAN-BUSINESS MODEL

Customers have two basic needs. *Human-Level*, the need to feel respected, cared for and to be treated as unique. *Business-Level*, the need to receive the product and service they have purchased. (see Figure 1.)

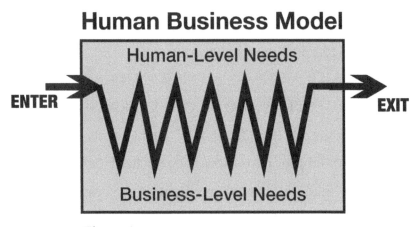

Figure 1

Customers want us to enter on the *Human-Level*, move down to the *Business-Level* rather quickly and move back and forth ending the transaction on the *Human-Level*.

## AN INTERACTION WITH MY LOCAL BANK

Teller: "Hey Greg, how are you?" (Start with Human-Level)

Greg: "Great! How are you doing?"

Teller: "We're doing fine. I hear Nicki (my wife) has gone back to be a flight attendant. That's exciting!" (Human-Level)

Greg: "Yes, she's excited. She flew once before and it was always her favorite job."

Teller: "That's great. Greg, what can I do for you today? (Business-Level)

Greg: "I need to take $1000 from savings and move it over to our checking account."

Teller: "My pleasure. Greg, do you have your account number with you? If not, I can pull it up here on the computer." (Business-Level)

*Notice how the teller responds, "My pleasure," and not, "No problem." I would suggest erasing "No problem" from your customer service vocabulary. "No problem" implies serving the customer could be a problem under other circumstances. Bottom line, the words we use are very important.*

Greg: "I don't have my account information with me. I'm sorry."

Teller: "I can look it up Greg. Where is Nicki going to be based?" (Human-Level)

Greg: "She'll be in Cincinnati."

Teller: "Found it Greg. Are you still at 185 Ash Brook?" (Business-Level)

Greg: "Yep, that's me."

Teller: "I've moved the $1000 from your savings over to your checking account. Please sign here." (Business-Level)

Teller: "Your kids still down in Bowling Green?" (Human-Level)

Greg: "Yes, they love Bowling Green."

Teller: "Bowling Green is a great town." (Human-Level)

Teller: "Greg, anything else I can help you with?" (Business-Level)

Greg: "No, that's it today."

Teller: "Great. Thanks Greg. Tell Nicki hello and that we're thinking of her." (Ends on Human-Level)


The key is to be authentic as you enter on the *Human-Level* versus a robotic, "Hello, what can I do for you?" and not really mean it. Generally, certain communication styles (Expressives & Amiables) desire more time on the *Human-Level* while certain communication styles (Drivers & Analyticals) typically desire more time on the *Business-Level*.

## QUESTIONS FOR CONSIDERATION

1. Why is entering on the Human-Level a challenge?

2. How can we ensure we don't sound and/or perceived as "robotic" when addressing the Human-Level needs?

3. Describe situations where we might spend too much time in one of the quadrants?

4. Why is important to go in and out each quadrant throughout the customer experience?

5. Why is it important to end the transaction at the Human-Level?

6. Why are the words we use important as related to customer service? What other responses ("No Problem") should be eliminated from our customer service vocabulary?

## MOMENT OF TRUTH

Jan Carlzon, former president and CEO of Scandinavia Airlines and author of "Moments of Truth" defines a Moment of Truth as any time the customer (or potential customer) comes into contact with any aspect of an organization, however remote, and has an opportunity to form an impression.

In my mind, there are two types of "Moments of Truth." Key "Moments of Truth" and Secondary "Moments of Truth." When I consult with organizations I have each department list Cycles of

Service (see Figure 2). Cycles of service are made up of "Moments of Truth," both "Key" and "Secondary." A "Secondary" Moment of Truth for an airline could be airport parking, even if they have little control of the parking. A "Key" Moment of Truth for an

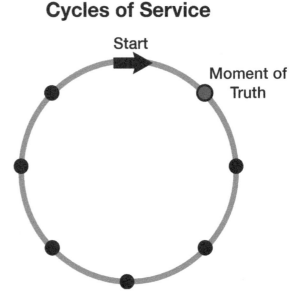

## Cycles of Service

Start

Moment of Truth

Figure 2

airline would be the ticket counter experience.

Service providers should put themselves in the shoes of the customers as they build a "Cycle of Service" for each department. Using the airline example, Ticketing, Flight Operations, Baggage, Reservations, et al would all have individual "Cycles of Service." Important questions: Is each step necessary? Could any step be eliminated? Streamlined? Strengthened? Are there "Moments of Truth" (parking) in which we have little or no control yet judged? What influence could be exerted for those "Moments of Truth" which we have little or no control?

## SUGGESTED ACTIVITY

1. List your organization's "Moments of Truth," both "Key" and "Secondary."

2. Build a "Cycle of Service" for each department within your business.

3. Is each step necessary? Could any step be eliminated? Streamlined? Strengthened? Are there "Moments of Truth" (parking) in which we have little control yet judged? What influence could be exerted for the "Moments of Truth" in which we have little or no control?

4. Debrief with your team on key lessons learned.

5. Develop an Action Plan of what key steps need to be taken to take your customer service to the next level.

## CUSTOMER REPORT CARD

Jan Carlzon defined a Moment of Truth as any time the customer (or potential customer) comes into contact with any aspect of an organization, however remote, and has an opportunity to form an impression. I would add, "and has an opportunity to grade our service." As elementary as it might seem, customers have a mental report card assigning a "grade" based on their experience (see Figure 3).

## Customer Report Card

| GRADE | EXPERIENCE |
|-------|------------|
| A | Knock Your Socks Off |
| B | Exceeded Expectations |
| C | As Expected |
| D | Victimized |
| F | Screwed |

Figure 3

If we provide a quality product, we're friendly, price is right; our customers will give us a C. That's what they expect! Bottom line, your customers will leave you for C service. No customer loyalty for C service! Occasionally when I travel I'll get off the interstate and take the back roads. I'm amazed at some of the signs I still see on the marquis. "Cable TV," Air Conditioning" are just a few examples of what customers would rate "C" while the service providers continue to think it's "A" service.

Today's "A" service will be tomorrow's "C" service, as customers get accustomed to a certain level of service and expect it from all others! We have to continuously be thinking of how we can provide "A" service to stay competitive and survive!

D service and the customer is walking out the door absent a proper "Recovery." F service, it's probably too late and the customer tells everyone he/she knows about your organization and their negative experience!

## QUESTIONS FOR CONSIDERATION

1. Overall, how would you "grade" your service?
2. How can you provide "A" and "B" service"
3. What products/services used to be "A" and/or "B" and now "C?"
4. How do you avoid "D" and "F" service?
5. How do you "Recover" from "D" and "F" service?

## THE COST OF A DISSATISFIED CUSTOMER

- Of those who complain, over half will come back if the compliant is resolved. Almost 100 percent will come back if the complaint is resolved quickly.
- Average customer with an unresolved compliant tells ten people about their experience.
- Average customer with a compliant that was resolved will only tell five about their experience.

Source: *White House Office of Consumer Affairs - The Cost of Poor Custmer Service" by Genesys Global Survey, 2009.*

## QUESTIONS FOR CONSIDERATION

1. What is the cost of a dissatisfied customer in your business?
2. What measures are in place to address dissatisfied customers?
3. Changes needed in your organization?

## SUGGESTED ACTIONS

1. Formal customer survey, focus groups, one-on-one interviews (include customers, vendors, employees, key stakeholders)
2. Implement a customer advisory board.
3. Invite customers to key meetings sharing their perceptions of your organization.
4. Invite end-users of your product/services to visit the front-line reminding employees the importance and value of their work. A consumer products company could invite a single mother to their factory to remind line workers the importance of what they do (providing her children a healthy lunch) and the people they serve.

# Chapter 27

## Problem Solving & Action Planning

### HELPFUL DEFINITIONS

- *Mission*-Purpose, reason for existing, core business.
- *Vision*-Future state, ideal state, what we're striving to be.
- *Goals*-A broad primary outcome.
- *Strategy*-The approach one takes to achieve a goal.
- *Objective*-A measurable step to achieve a strategy.
- *Tactics*-A tool used in pursuing an objective associated with a defined strategy.
- *Consensus*-Can I live with it? Can I support?
- *Facilitator*-Content neutral, process servant to a team.

## EXAMPLE

Mission: To provide tools that fuel America's Automotive Manufacturers.

Vision: We will be the customer's first choice when selecting tools for the automotive manufacturing industry while being viewed as the subject matter experts.

Goal: To Make Acme Tool Company a leader in the Tool & Die industry.

Strategy: Convince buyers that Acme Tools are the best by associating and co-branding with established manufacturers.

Objective: Retain a 35 percent market share in the automotive supply business according to the Lane Index Report.

Tactic: Participate in all North American tradeshows in 2016.

## STRATEGIC PLANNING AND PROBLEM SOLVING

I regularly get calls inquiring about my planning workshops and retreats. It usually comes from someone who's heard participants actually walk away from my sessions somewhat refreshed and excited about the future. They report past strategic planning and problem-solving sessions that resulted in an increase of calls to mental health clinics. The problem is that most people and organizations don't understand there are two types of meetings and planning sessions.

## TWO TYPES OF MEETINGS

The first and most common meeting is one that is conducted. It is characterized by one-way communication and information dissemination by a single person. The focus is compliance to an agenda versus commitment to an outcome. The second type of meeting is one that is facilitated. It's characterized by two-way communication, input and buy-in to the agenda. The facilitator is more of a coach versus conductor with a goal of participation and input from all participants. While many report, "facilitating" meetings, they've actually conducted them. Ideally, strategic planning sessions are facilitated.

## TWO TYPES PLANNING SESSIONS

The first type of planning/problem-solving session (flying at 1000 feet) is characterized by a much smarter person than me facilitating a team/organization through an extremely academic, through and lengthy process with the outcome a very large and impressive binder(s). These sessions can be important in securing grants, providing regulators/auditors with very important information as well as providing direction and accountability to a board, leadership team, et al.

I have the deepest respect for this type of planning/problem-solving and logic would say a team/organization/board should start here. And very often, they should. But way too often, a team/board/ organization is not ready, mentally nor physically. Mentally, they've not been properly briefed as to the time and commitment necessary for success. As a result, team members are often "gun shy" for future sessions. Worst, an impressive, expensive and underutilized binder(s) sits on a credenza simply collecting dust.

The second type of planning/problem-solving (30,000 feet) is where I suggest teams/organizations/boards start. This session is typically shorter, more informal and less granular than the first. This session can serve as both a stand-alone session and a warm-up for a more formal session if deemed necessary.

The following is an overview of a planning model with its genesis a chamber of commerce who needed someone to facilitate a "Program of Work" for that particular year. They had several limitations: The session needed to be a short day. Board members, while committed, would have trouble staying engaged if it went too deep. And lastly, it needed to be an informal, retreat like setting.

## THE PLANNING MODEL

The first question I ask, "Does your organization have a mission and vision?" The most common response is, "Yes, but we've not reviewed in many years." Naturally, I suggest starting the session with mission and vision revisitation and/or creation. If it's an intact team and without responsibility for mission and vision development and/ or they feel comfortable with their current mission and vision, we start with the actual problem solving.

## GETTING STARTED:
## NECESSARY ITEMS FOR A PLANNING SESSION

- Easel Stands (get good sturdy ones versus wobbly music stands)
- Easel Pads (Post-It® Note brand that sticks to wall works well)
- Masking Tape (even with the Post-It® Note brand, you will find the need to reinforce after several removals)
- Colored Markers (the variety of color is easy on the eyes. The scented ones work best)
- Post-It® Notes for multi-voting (a variety of colors and sizes)
- Paper/Pen (for those that come unprepared)

## MISSION & VISION

Whatever you determine should be on the agenda, I strongly suggest a pre-workshop packet sent to all participants at least one week prior to the session. Contents should be the current mission and vision, pertinent organizational information and clear directions on what, if anything, participants need to do prior to session. Unfortunately, assume the majority will never review the contents.

Assuming the organization has a mission and vision, the first step is distribute (they should have a copy in their pre-workshop packet) a copy of the mission and vision determining if changes are needed. Most teams elect to modify due to the time elapsed since the last review and/or new developments in the organization/industry.

Traditionally, most organizations created an individual mission (purpose for existing, usually and ideally one sentence) and vision (future state, motherhood, apple pie and Chevrolet). Today, many organizations create one single document that's a combination of both mission and vision.

## THE ROLE OF THE FACILITATOR
### *A Facilitator: 100 percent content neutral and a process servant to a team.*

When I consult with organizations I'm about as close to this definition as one can be. I'm usually an outsider and while I have a sincere interest in their success, after the session I go home. Realistically, you may be asked to "facilitate" for either your team and/or a team within your organization. Naturally, if you're a member of that team/organization, you will not be 100 percent content neutral. You will have ideas/thoughts and occasionally need to share those thoughts/ideas.

## FACILITATOR AS PARTICIPANT

During the beginning of the meeting when securing consensus on "Roles," simply ask permission to step out of role as facilitator when you feel it necessary to share your thoughts/ideas. Let's say you're list building and standing beside the easel with marker in hand. Psychologically, when you're up front, with marker in hand, you're perceived as the leader of the group. The last thing you want to do, as a facilitator is to "lead" the group in any one direction.

If you must add to the discussion, communicate the following: "Team, as we discussed at the beginning of the meeting, there may be times I feel the need to temporarily leave my role as facilitator and participate. You granted me permission to step out of role and I would like to do that now." Put the marker down and have a seat with your team. Make your comments, conclude and then resume your position as the facilitator.

## THE PROCESS

Assuming the decision is to consider one document (mission & vision combination), I give each participant a few minutes individually to review the current mission and vision. Instruct participants to circle key words and make note of words/phrases/concepts/principles that are noticeably missing. This could be the case if there's been substantial industry/organizational change since the original drafting. The individual time is important, as most participants need time to process prior to group activity, which is the next step.

## SUBGROUPING

After a few minutes individually, I place participants into subgroups. Each subgroup's task is to come to consensus on one mission/vision statement. The ideal subgroup size is between 6-8 participants. If your team is less than 5-6, there's no need for subgrouping. The rationale for subgrouping is it's easier to come to consensus with 5-6 participants than with 10-15.

The directions for the subgroups includes having each individual share thoughts about the current mission and vision, key words that are important, words/phrases that are absent, how they might modify. After each participant shares his/her thoughts, the subgroup should move toward creating one mission/vision for that subgroup. I provide each subgroup an easel pad, markers, masking tape. Each subgroup selects a spokesperson, places (Post-It® Note Easel Pads work well for this simply tearing off a sheet for each subgroup) the completed document on the wall. This part of the exercise usually takes approximately 15-20 minutes depending on the size of the group.

Because individuals are by nature competitive, subgroups will have created an "Our mission/vision is better than yours!" mentality. Remind participants the reason for placing participants into subgroups: Easier to achieve consensus with 5-6 than with 10-15. Challenge the team to forget about subgroup membership and unite, taking the best of the 3-4 draft mission/vision statements coalescing around one for the entire team/organization.

Place easel sheets side-by-side and have each subgroup spokesperson stand and read for the entire group. After each, challenge the group to note key words/phrases they feel should be included in a final draft. After all have been reviewed, a final draft emerges (one or two participants typically take the lead in creating the final document). This part of the process usually takes approximately 30-45 minutes.

In approximately one hour, most teams/organizations can successful revisit, update and make the appropriate modifications to their mission/vision statements. Assuming a team/organization rarely has 100 percent participation in a planning session, it is important to view all outcomes as "Drafts." Post session; communicate to all members soliciting feedback before finalizing future plans and documents. Absent team members will appreciate the inclusion and this sign of solidarity will prove strategic.

In a situation where a team/organization/board is creating a mission and vision for the first time, I basically use the same process, spending more time defining mission and vision as well as distinguishing major differences between the two. In the pre-session packet, consider benchmarking similar boards/organizations with sample mission and vision statements.

While I have facilitated sessions with the sole agenda item being mission and vision creation/revisitation, most sessions include a problem solving and action-planning component. If this is the case, encourage participants in the pre-session packet to be thinking about specific issues to be discussed and/or that are holding the team/organization back.

As a facilitator, it is important to monitor energy and commitment levels. Even if the initial plan was to transition to a problem-solving session and you sense low energy and/or commitment, articulate this observation and make a group decision on moving forward or regrouping at a later time.

## TRANSITIONING FROM MISSION/VISION TO PROBLEM-SOLVING

**Going Well & Getting Stuck**

Naturally, a team will want to immediately start with the negative, specifically what's holding them back. I encourage teams/ organizations/boards to first identify what's going well. This will do three things. One, it starts the problem solving session on a positive note. Two, it serves as an appreciation for a job well done for individuals responsible for particular areas within the organization. Thirdly, it serves as a foundation for the next phase of "where are we getting stuck" as very often what is perceived to be "going well" could also be an area of improvement.

## GOING WELL

Just as with mission/vision, give participants a few minutes individually to process before building the "Going Well" list.  After a few minutes, start with building the list using two easel stands, easel pad with "Going Well" across the top and two different colored markers to alternate between each item. Rather than traditional "Brainstorming," where you simply open it up and participants randomly shout out their thoughts, I suggest using a process called "Round Robin."

With "Round Robin" each participant systematically offers one item off his/her list. As with traditional "Brainstorming," no explanation and/or clarification are needed at this point. Challenge participants to give you their thoughts/ideas in three to four words versus long sentences. This will serve you well as you're boarding and clarifying once the list is built. After each idea/thought respond with a, "Thank you," versus random value judgments ("good suggestion!") on certain ideas/thoughts protecting you from embarrassment when a participant says something really stupid (and they will) and you can't say anything positive.

Instruct participants that once an idea/thought has been spoken and placed on the easel simply mark it off their list. There's no need to repeat that item. If a participant doesn't have an item to share instruct them to simply say, "Pass." Once it's apparent most participants are passing, open it up to traditional "Brainstorming" where participants who have items left simply communicate them for recording.

The rationale for starting with "Round Robin" versus traditional "Brainstorming" is with Round Robin everyone has an equal opportunity for participation versus one or two dominant participants monopolizing. It also gives the reticent team member a less threatening avenue to participate. Once the list is complete, it's now time for explanation and/or clarification.

Simply run a hand down each item repeating the item and instructing participants to ask for explanation and/or clarification if needed. If needed, ask the participant responsible for that item to provide explanation and/or clarification. Caution: Don't spend too much time on the "Going Well." Few will argue with the list and the majority of time and energy should be dedicated to the next portion (Getting Stuck).

## GETTING STUCK

As related to roadblocks and problems, many teams/organizations/boards are stuck simply not knowing where to start, so they don't! They're overwhelmed and if/when there's motivation to get started, differing opinions on where to start tends to be subjective which often leads to team/organizational conflict. Stephen Covey said it best, "No involvement, no commitment." Without involvement you'll get compliance but not commitment.

## THE PROCESS

As with the earlier list building, give each participant a few minutes to process. Be prepared to let this go a little longer than the previous "Going Well." In fact, be prepared for this entire process taking substantially longer. Build the list using Round Robin transitioning to Brain Storming when most start to pass. Number each item as this makes the eventual combination and categorization much easier. Again, solicit three to four word descriptions versus long rambling sentences. Simply build the list assuring participants they will have an opportunity for clarification after all items are boarded.

## CLARIFICATION

Once the list is built, the next step is to clarify any necessary items. Simply run your hand down each item asking participants to stop you when they need clarification on a particular item. When someone stops and needs clarification ask, "Whose item is this?" Once identified simply ask for clarification. The key is clarification, not selling and/or building the case for that particular idea/thought. They will have this opportunity if their idea/thought is selected later in the process.

Many teams get stuck at this point as they see a large list, become overwhelmed and adjourn with little or no progress. A facilitator's role is to assist in whittling that list of 30-40 "Getting Stuck" items down to something more manageable. Remember, "An elephant can be eaten one bite at a time."

## WHITTLING THE LIST DOWN

### Elimination, Combination and Categorization

By design, brainstorming encourages participants to put as many ideas/thoughts for consideration on the table. If a team has been successful in building an unrestricted list there will be a need for eliminating certain items. Simply run your hand down the list as in the clarification stage asking for any items/thoughts the entire team agrees should be eliminated. If a single participant disagrees with eliminating a particular item, leave the item on the list. Not to worry, the likelihood of that item getting a hearing will be minimum.

## COMBINATION

The next phase is to look for opportunities for combination. Simply ask participants to look at the list and see if opportunities exist for combination. Numbering the items as suggested earlier will make this much easier as you can use a separate easel sheet and simply use the number versus having to rewrite the entire idea/thought. For example, there may be four items that refer to a particular subject. Simply combining those four items into one starts to clean the list up and most importantly makes that list more manageable.

## CATEGORIZATION

Next, encourage participants to look for opportunities for categorization. For example, if a team had dorms, off-campus housing, and physical plant as individual items they may elect to categorize as simply, "Facilities." In my experience, by the time you get to this phase the original list of 30-40 has been whittled down to 10-15 items. At this point there will be crossed out items and new categories documented on pretty messy easel sheets necessitating a break to organize and clean up the list.

After the break, participants should see all original items either grouped under individual categories or standing alone as they did when originally posted. It is important to communicate the integrity of the process by ensuring participants all items/thoughts will be considered. You've simply made the list more manageable with the tools of elimination, combination and categorization. Save all work documents (easel pads) for future reference and/or aids in preparing final report.

## DECIDING WHERE TO BEGIN

Congratulations, you've assisted a team in identifying growth areas and taken a large and unmanageable list and turned it into a narrowed and more manageable list of growth areas. Let's say you've managed to get that list of 30-40 items down to 15 items. Unless you have several days dedicated for a planning session (most don't) 15 items will be impossible to tackle. The challenge is to prioritize the 15 items into 3-5 items that can be addressed in the remaining time, in my experience usually only a few hours.

## MULTI-VOTING

At this point, I will ask the team, "I have a tool called Multi-Voting designed to assist a team prioritize the top 3-4 items as related to where we might start the problem-solving process. Would you be interested in learning how this process works?" I've never had a refusal at this point so I explain.

## MULTI-VOTING DIRECTIONS

- Distribute each participant three Post-It® Notes. (Why three? Any more than three there's a danger of one or two enterprising participants joining together combining Post-It® Notes on a particular item(s) creating an appearance of widespread interest).

- Participants can place and distribute Post-It® Notes on any item(s) they deem to be the most important. For instance, if a participant feels a particular item is important, he/she can place all three Post-It® Notes on that item. Or he/she can place two on that item and the third on another item. Or simply place a Post-It® Note on three different items.

- Suggest participants write the item number on the Post-It® Note in case it falls to ground before the votes are tallied.

- Strongly communicate that all items will be addressed at some point. We're simply identifying the three or four items that appear to be getting the most attention at this point in time. Remaining items will be carried over to a future planning session. Avoid a "winners" and "losers" mentality.

- I often find that once a team identifies the top three or four items the remaining items fall into place as subsets of the three or four.

- Have participants place their Post-It® Notes on the item(s) they deem most important.

- Once all participants have distributed their Post-It® Notes, count each one for each item.

- Within a few minutes, the top three or four items will emerge.

- Debrief the experience. Surprises?

## DECISION TO MOVE FORWARD

It is important to monitor the energy of your participants. This entire process is both mentally and physically draining. Many teams will have had enough at this point. They've created/revisited a mission/vision, identified organizational strengths, organizational growth areas, eliminated, combined, categorized and participated in thought provoking discussions. Many elect to take the results of this session to their next board meeting and start the problem solving and action planning at a later date. I understand this decision. Some however decide to continue by taking the three-four items from the Multi-Voting and start problem solving and action planning.

## CRITERIA

Decisions that are perceived to be subjective are almost guaranteed to result in conflict. Decisions that are perceived to be objective are less likely to result in conflict and more easily explained and justified in the future. The use of criteria can be a useful tool for a facilitator.

"Criteria: a standard, rule, or test on which a judgment or decision can be based."

Source: Merriam-Webster Dictionary

For example, you're the chairman of the board of an association that's been charged with hiring an executive director. While your team has received hundreds of resumes, several are local with political connections. Realizing the ultimate decision will be questioned, you suggest developing a list of criteria of the ideal candidate (education, experience, industry knowledge, financial background, knowledge of area, etc.) with each criterion weighted based on importance.

Each finalist is evaluated, ranked and compared to other applicants based on the objective criteria with the hiring decision based on this through analysis. As predicted, the selection of the new executive director is questioned by not only local community members but members of your association. Your response to questions regarding your hiring decision might sound like this:

"Thank you for your interest in our association and the new executive director. We had an impressive list of candidates and our decision was a difficult one. As an association, we developed criteria we felt most important in an executive director. We weighted each criterion and evaluated each candidate based on those criteria. The decision was an objective one and we are excited about the future."

While hundreds of problem solving models exist, our goal is to keep it simple. Google GBASS problem solving model and nothing will pop up. I wish I could take credit for it but I can't. In fact, I'm not sure to whom credit should be given. The urban legend is that a front line utility worker was in one of my colleague's class and commented that most problem-solving models boiled down to GBASS. Perplexed, my colleague asked, "GBASS, What's GBASS?" His response, "All problem solving models seem to have five things in common. The goal, barriers to reaching that goal, alternatives that might work, selecting from those alternatives and finally determining the sequence of those things you've decided to do. GBASS." He was right!

GBASS *Goal:* Many find it easier if the goal is phrased in the form of a question. For instance, if one of the issues from the Multi-Voting is "Marketing," the goal could be, "How do we create an effective marketing program?"

*Barriers*: As facilitator, use Brainstorming to build a list of the barriers that could keep you from reaching your goal. Be careful not to spend too much time on barriers. The idea is to identify and move quickly. Using the above example, participants might identify lack of a budget, no real expertise, crowded market, etc. After the list is built, challenge participants to determine which barriers can be controlled and/or influenced. Don't get bogged down on the ones you have no control and/or influence.

*Alternatives*. Brainstorm a list of alternatives (ideas) on how to reach the goal of creating an effective marketing program while considering identified barriers. Using the example of creating an effective marketing program, alternatives might include: benchmarking industry leaders, hiring marketing consultant, research past marketing efforts, identify stakeholders and customers, survey current customers, focus groups, etc.

*Select*: Using the above list, facilitate participants in selecting which items they would like to pursue. It could be as simple as coming to consensus with an informal discussion or as formal as using Multi-Voting. I typically let the team decide without the use of formal facilitation tools. Be careful not to use facilitation tools just for the sake of using them.

*Sequence*: This is this is the most important part of GBASS. This is the Action-Planning part of the model. Take the items from the above Select phase and place on a traditional Action Plan (What/Who/When). I'm a pretty responsible person but if leave a session and my name is not on an Action Plan, it will not get done.

## AN OUTLINE FOR A SUCCESSFUL MEETING

Whether you're asked to facilitate or conduct a meeting, I would suggest always starting with the following on a flip chart as participants enter the room: Outcome Statement, Agenda, Roles, Norms, Parking Lot, and Action Plan.

If it's a traditional meeting that you conduct versus facilitate, simply review the items and get started. Consider sending out a copy of the Outcome Statement, etc. before the meeting via email and/or traditional mail.

## OUTCOME

*Outcome:* I always start the Outcome Statement with, "At the end of this meeting (the time you commit to ending the meeting), we will have (fill in with what you hope to achieve)."

*Sample Outcome Statement*: At the end of this meeting (5pm), we will have identified ideas to improve our company's involvement in the communities we serve across the state. Additionally, we will have created an Action Plan based upon the agreed upon ideas.

*What you might say if it's a meeting that's being conducted*: "The following is our outcome for our meeting this afternoon."

*What you might say if the meeting is facilitated*: "The following is what I perceive to be the outcome of our meeting this afternoon. Do you agree if we can meet this outcome by 5pm it will have been a good use of our time?"

If you've done your homework and involved others in the creation of the Outcome Statement, you will rarely have anyone say, "No, I don't think it will be a good use of our time." But if you're truly "facilitating," you must be ready for this. If it happens, simply ask, "Ok, specifically what would you suggest we change?" Regroup, get consensus and move on.

## AGENDA

*Agenda:* A simple list of how we will reach the Outcome Statement? I typically use the following statement as a transition from Outcome Statement to Agenda, "If the Outcome is the destination, let's take a look at a road map in the form of an Agenda."

## SAMPLE AGENDA

- Getting Started (Outcome, Agenda, Roles, Norms, Parking Lot, Action Plan)
- Round Robin/Brainstorming ideas to reach the outcome
- Clarify List
- Combination and Categorization
- Select Alternatives
- Action Plan
- Debrief/Next Steps
- Adjourn

*What you might say if the meeting is conducted*: "The following is our agenda for the afternoon. Questions?"

*What you might say if the meeting is facilitated:* "Do you feel this agenda will work in helping us reach the outcome we just outlined?"

Again, if you've done your homework and involved others in creating the agenda, you will rarely have anyone say, "No, I don't think this agenda will work" But if you're truly "facilitating," you must be ready for this. If it happens, simply ask, "Ok, specifically what would you suggest we change in the agenda?" Regroup, get consensus and move on.

## ROLES

*Roles:* Your role as either facilitator or meeting leader and participant roles as meeting participants.

## SAMPLE

* Your Role: Active participants sharing your thoughts, ideas, concerns for moving forward (opposite of warm buns in seats)
* My Role:
  1. Meeting Leader (if conducting the meeting); or
  2. My Role: Meeting Facilitator (if facilitating). (I also define facilitator on this easel sheet as "Facilitator: Content Neutral/ Process Servant To Your Team)

*What you might say if the meeting is conducted*: "Here's how I see our roles for this afternoon's meeting."

*What you might say if the meeting is facilitated:* "Here's how I see your role for this afternoon's meeting. Are you ok with your role? Can you live up to your role?"

"What about my role as facilitator? The way I define facilitator is Content Neutral – I'm not going to get in your business; Process Servant – my job is to help you reach your outcome in the most timely and efficient manner. I have several tools to assist with this.

Is everyone ok with my role as facilitator? Will you be ok with me intervening if I perceive we're getting stuck?"

## NORMS

*Norms:* Guidelines of how we can best work together during this meeting.

## SAMPLE

- Full participation
- Attack issues – not people
- Confidentiality
- Monitor team's time (come back from breaks on time)
- Think outside the 9 Dots (creativity)

*What you might say if the meeting is conducted:* "Here are some Norms that I suggest we try to live up to during our meeting this afternoon."

*What you might say if the meeting is facilitated:* "I have found that in successful meetings it is important we all agree upon a few norms of how we're going to work together. I've taken the liberty of jotting a few down. Let's review . . . Any you would want to add? Delete?" Can we all commit to living up to these Norms?

## PARKING LOT

*Parking Lot*: In most meetings, there will participants who bring up a topic that may be important but not the appropriate time to discuss. Because you want to respect the person introducing the topic and make sure it's addressed at a more appropriate time, an easel sheet with the word "Parking Lot" written across the top can be very helpful. It basically works the same for both conducted and facilitated meetings.

*What you might say*: "Because there will most likely be times when someone introduces an idea that may be important but it's not the most appropriate time to discuss. We want to make sure it doesn't get lost by not addressing at that time, I suggest when this happens we write the idea in the "Parking Lot." At any time we perceive this happening, simply make the suggestion, walk over to the easel sheet labeled "Parking Lot," and write that item on it. I promise, before we adjourn we will address each item on the Parking Lot."

## ACTION PLAN

*Action Plan*: A simple matrix outlining what is to be accomplished, who will be responsible for that particular item, and when an update will be given on progress and/or completion.

## WARNING

I am a pretty responsible person, but if my name isn't on an Action Plan when I leave a meeting, it will not get done! If you leave a meeting, whether conducted or facilitated, and do not have an Action Plan with deliverables, participant's names, timelines, you're fooling yourself if you think anything will get done!

*What you might say*: "Before we leave here today, we will have numerous items on an Action Plan that highlights the What, the Who and the When. On the wall, you will see an easel sheet that serves as an example."

## IT'S NOT THE X'S & O'S, IT'S THE JIM & JOE'S (AND JANE'S)

My friend Terry Obee and I were recently discussing the importance and key components of strategic planning. I was making my case for a methodical approach to planning while taking advantage of numerous time-tested planning models. I referenced SWOT analysis where a team identifies Strengths, Weaknesses, Opportunities, and Threats. I also mentioned a model where a team simply answers three basic questions:

1. What's going well?
2. Where are we getting stuck?
3. What should we be doing differently?

These planning models and my general philosophy on strategic planning I shared with Terry Obee that day were based on more than twenty-years of consulting with hundreds of teams and organizations. I peppered the conversation with quotes like, "Fail to plan, plan to fail," and "Measure twice and cut once." Engaged, Terry simply listened. But what he said after my academic rambling was indeed provocative and based on his experience as a professional athlete playing for the Chicago Bears and the legendary Mike Ditka.

Confidently, Terry said, *"Greg, it's not the X's & Os, it's the Jim & Joe's."* I could instantly visualize the many binders in my office that contained the most sophisticated of all plans. Plans with charts, references, guidelines, timelines, goals, strategies, tactics, etc. Most of those binders, all filled with the "X's& O's," were simply collecting dust as the "Jim & Joe's" were neither identified and/or not committed or even worse not held accountable to the execution of these well thought out plans.

Terry and I both agreed planning models and a systematic approach are important. But perhaps the most important piece of the puzzle is the one that follows the actual planning process. A simple Action Plan. An Action Plan consisting of: What (X's & O's), Who (Jim & Joe's) and When (Timeline). Ironically, the reason most plans never get off the ground is because we don't take the time at the conclusion of a meeting to complete the most elementary of all models. A basic Action Plan that in addition to identifying the X's & O's identifies the "Jim & Joe's."

And like you, I'm a pretty responsible person. However, if my name doesn't appear on an Action Plan, the odds of me or anyone else following through are slim to none! Even with the best of intentions, we're busy people. We're excited and committed when we leave the planning session but then life resumes. We assume someone else will do it (staff, executive director, board members or board chair). But if we know an Action Plan will be posted at the next meeting with actual names and timelines, you better believe we will follow through!

An effective leader balances the "X's & O's" with the "Jim & Joe's." How many times have we shared a plan with others who weren't involved and didn't have a role in the development of that plan only to be surprised when they weren't overly excited or 100 percent committed during the implementation phase? Steven Covey, author of "The Seven Habits of Highly Effective People" knew the importance of including the "Jim & Joe's" when he said, "No involvement; no commitment." But my friend Terry Obee simplified things even further with a sports analogy. "It's not the X's & O's, it's the Jim & Joe's (and Jane's)."

## SETTING YOUR ANCHOR

I've boated much of my adult life. I inherited a small fishing boat from a neighbor who was my nautical mentor. My second boat was an 18-foot ski boat, eventually graduating to a 21-foot run-about. While each boat had an anchor, it didn't get much use as the lake where we boated was very deep and throwing an anchor overboard proved pointless. In addition to depth, the bottom of the lake was littered with debris because it had not been cleared before flooding. The intent was to create a source of water for an electric generation plant, only later becoming a source of recreation.

After being out of the boating business for several years, my wife and I decided to purchase a 27-foot Cruiser. After getting our new boat in the water, a friend of mine informed me that I didn't have the proper anchor. So, I bought a new anchor, connected it to 150-feet of rope and threw it overboard. I felt it hit the bottom and tied the remaining rope on the nearest cleat.

Settled into a cove several hundred feet from the bank, I turned on the music and stretched out for a little R & R. Just as I closed my eyes, I heard my wife scream, "We're on the bank!" What just happened, I thought. I had felt the anchor hit bottom and knew I had more than enough rope. I pulled the anchor up, started the engine and cruised back to our original spot. Once again, I dropped anchor and within just a few short minutes, I heard my wife yell, "We're on the bank again!"

A few weeks later, I had a conversation with a friend with much more experience in the boating business than me. After describing my dilemma, my friend asked, "Do you have a chain attached to your anchor?" "A chain?" I asked. "I had what I thought was the proper anchor and 150-feet of new marine-grade rope." My friend explained that without the weight of a few feet of chain, my anchor was never "setting." It was simply dangling around the lake floor and never serving its intended purpose.

## THE ANCHOR, THE ROPE, THE CHAIN, THE BOTTOM & THE VESSEL

Like many unexpected and seemingly unimportant events, my boating situation can teach us quite a bit about the strategic direction of our organization. The associated metaphors can be the glue for both internalization of key concepts and a valuable tool for sharing these important organizational lessons with others.

## THE ANCHOR

When I think of an anchor I think of stability. An anchor is something that keeps us grounded. In an organization, it's our mission and vision. An anchor can be our company values, our history, our culture, and our purpose for existing.

## KEY QUESTIONS

1. Do we know the anchors of our organization?
2. Do we think about them on a regular basis?
3. Do they provide the focus needed to serve others?
4. Are our anchors inspirational?
5. Do they ground us?
6. Do we schedule enough time communicating our anchors with employees, customers, investors, and board members?

## THE ROPE

The rope connects us to the anchor. Tiny strands bonding together, intertwined, becoming stronger and stronger. From an organizational perspective, it's our employees, our investors, our customers, and our leadership team. The rope represents our policies, procedures, our goals, and objectives. When I purchased the 150-feet of rope for my boat, I remember the salesperson explaining the importance of "marine-grade" rope. "Not just any rope would do!" he exclaimed.

## KEY QUESTIONS

1.  Is our organizational rope "marine-grade?"
2.  Do we occasionally lower our standards and cut corners out of convenience, time and budget constraints?
3.  How strong is our rope?
4.  What kind of job are we doing intertwining individual strands to make our initiatives and key business strategies as strong as possible?
5.  Is our rope long enough? Is it attached to the anchor?
6.  Are there knots in the form of organizational obstacles in our rope?
7.  If so, what are the major causes of organizational knots?
8.  Are they easily untangled?

## THE CHAIN

The chain sets the anchor. In a sense, the chain is the most important, but often the most overlooked, part of the trio. One might experience moderate success, albeit short-lived, without the chain. When I tossed my anchor without the chain, the weight of the anchor and the calmness of the water gave me an impression of success. But when the winds picked up and the currents changed, we were on the bank. Organizationally, what happens when the winds pick up and the currents change?

The chain includes the empowerment of our employees. It's the power of engagement. It's the trust we have in our employees and they in us. It's the ownership our team feels as a result of having input in the direction of the organization. The chain is the culture we've worked so hard to create, maintain and channel into peak performance. It's our mission, vision, goals, and objectives coming alive. It's teamwork (many strands intertwined) and the sense of appreciation between all team members. And without the chain, our anchor is simply dangling around the water's floor never serving its intended purpose.

## KEY QUESTIONS

1. Does your organization have a chain?

2. What happens when the organizational winds pick up and the currents change?

3. Have you been drifting with the currents of change, or setting a steady course?

4. Have you experienced success in spite of not properly setting your anchor?

5. Can that success be sustained?

6. How much is not having a chain costing your organization; or one that is not strong and appropriately linked?

## THE BOTTOM

The major reason I never considered using an anchor during my early boating years was the depth of the lake and the condition of the bottom. The local utility company never envisioned the lake for recreational use. They simply flooded the river creating a water supply for electric generation. The result was rotting trees, barns and other debris just below the surface making for hazardous conditions. Over the years, thousands of boaters have cut their rope after realizing their anchor was tangled in the sunken detritus.

## KEY QUESTIONS

1. What does your organizational bottom, your competitive landscape, look like?

2. Depending on what's at the bottom, marine experts recommend different types of anchors.

3. Is the bottom muddy or is it sandy? A rocky bottom or one littered with shipwrecks?

4. Do you consider what's on the bottom before choosing anchors?

5. From a market perspective, do you spend enough time evaluating the waterways before launching your vessel?

6. And when do you know it's time to "cut the rope?"

## THE VESSEL

What's the condition of your vessel, your organization? While we did some "due diligence" before purchasing our boat, we recently discovered a leak in the fuel tank. Additionally, the mechanic noted a few concerns with our engine. Both issues will prove costly and steal our time away from the lake.

## KEY QUESTIONS

1. Should we have done a better job in our "due diligence?"
2. Did our boat advisors steer us in the right direction?
3. Could these problems have been identified before we decided to purchase?
4. How much will the repairs cost?
5. What preventive maintenance measures should be taken moving forward?
6. What future investments should be made?
7. Should we even be in the boat business?
8. Do we have a "rainy day" fund for unexpected expenses?
9. How long will we be out of commission?
10. How much does the time away from the lake really cost?

These setbacks have definitely made our family more cognizant of the condition of our vessel. But most importantly, it has made us more aware of the changes we need to make our journeys both safe and enjoyable. Bon Voyage!

# Chapter 28

## Organizational Dynamics

### GOVERNANCE/STRUCTURE

A friend relays a story of asking his child if he knew how much a broken lamp cost – shortly after it was knocked off an end table. His son's response, "No, you've never told me." We make similar assumptions in the workplace. I've worked with three Fortune 500 companies and was never formally briefed on corporate governance. But, I learned pretty quickly that when a board member was in town, our entire office was cleaned like never before, and the entire management team on edge for days before the official visit.

Organizational governance is a term that refers broadly to the rules, processes, or bylaws by which organizations are operated, regulated, and controlled. There is usually a governing board of directors (public companies), officers (banks), cabinet secretaries (government), owners (private business), school board members (public schools), and boards of regents (college/universities).

From a Soft Skills perspective, offering assistance to your immediate supervisor and management team when a board member or a member of senior management is to visit your facility is a career-enhancing move. From a management perspective, educating your employees on governance and structure, the value board members play and how they fit into organizational structure is not only a leader's responsibility but also an opportunity for engaging and involving employees.

## LEVELS/HIERARCHY

Organizations are paradoxes. They're wonderful places; they're horrible places. They build employees up; they tear employees down. They're good for one's self-confidence; they're the reason many are in therapy. Because most organizations model their structure and governance from military operations, they tend to be both autocratic and hierarchical in nature. One of the most blatant forms of an organizational caste system is the level placed on employees that determine pay and responsibility.

I hadn't been on my first job but a few days when I was introduced as a "pay grade 4 staff manager." My boss was a pay grade 5. When I was teaching at our company's Management Institute, my supervisors in my class often referred to me as a "second level." There were even predictions related to levels and pay grade that if someone didn't make it to a particular level by a certain age then it would never happen.

And it's not just corporate America that's obsessed with levels and where everyone fits. I spent a few years in state government and while not all divisions are as clearly defined, everyone's salaries are public knowledge and published in the local newspaper. Although it's less obvious in private business, power structures and pecking orders clearly exist

Be aware of organizational dynamics without becoming obsessed with where you are and where you desire to be. As a leader, demystify pay grade levels and the titles that divide. Don't wear your position on your sleeve. Employees are keenly aware of who's in charge and where they fall in the organizational hierarchy. Pay close attention to the subtle signs that discriminate (parking, perks). Keep your head down and do the best job you can do. You'll be noticed and get ahead.

## CHAIN OF COMMAND

I was fresh out of college and accepted a position with a major trucking company as a management trainee. I was assigned to a rural terminal and felt isolated most of time. Full of myself, I was scheduled for a training program at division headquarters. Taking advantage of being where senior management resided, I dropped by a division vice president's office and confidently introduced myself, and expressed my interest in moving up in the company.

While I don't remember much of that encounter with the vice president, I remember the meeting (or should I say butt-chewing) that followed when I returned to my job at the rural terminal. It wasn't my supervisor who called me into his office, but rather his boss's boss who stopped by and asked to see me. He closed the door and said, "Son, if you weren't young, dumb and stupid, I would fire your butt right now! I assume you've never heard of the chain of command because you just broke it during your little trip. You went several levels above my head and if ever happens again I will personally send you packing!"

Bottom line; never break the chain of command!

There's a balance somewhere between never letting people know what you want and the other extreme of over lobbying. Unfortunately, I have been right of center most of my life. My Driver/Expressive personality has been both an asset and a liability in letting others know what I want. While not a partisan, former Vice President Al Gore and President George Bush serve as examples. Al Gore is perceived to have wanted to become president since he was born, while George Bush is perceived to have wanted to be a cowboy, policeman and firefighter. In short, the one who over lobbies rarely

# Avoid Over Lobbying

Never Letting Anyone Know                     Over Lobbying

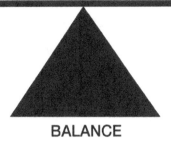

**BALANCE**

gets the job and the one who "low keys it" usually ends up with the position.

Timing also plays a part in job opportunity and selection. A friend of mine is fond of saying, "You don't pick history; history picks you." Again, using a political example absent partisanship, who would have predicted George Bush would be reelected to a second term? But then entered 9-11; and Bush's response sealed his re-election. I'm still surprised Barack Obama was elected the first time given his inexperience, but timing is indeed everything. America was ready for an African American president, coupled with his personal appeal; all of which propelled him into the White House. The stars must indeed be in total alignment for anyone to be elected!

## YOUR NEXT MOVE

Staying in a job position for at least three years before lobbying for another position seems to be an accepted timeframe. I asked my friend, a high-ranking military general, what was the key to his success? Humbly he responded, "I've always done the job assigned to me to the best of my ability without thinking of my next move or opportunity." Sage advice indeed!

## GETTING AHEAD

Riding in a subway car with the president of our company, I asked, "What does it take to get ahead in this company?" With little hesitation he replied, "Two things: (1) You have to be smart, and (2) You have to have a sponsor!" From his response and my gut, I suspected the latter was more important than the former. Well, I was smart enough and I had a sponsor. Even though he was not the president, my sponsor was a well-respected vice president with whom I developed a relationship early in my career. Realizing I had an interest in politics and a background in Washington DC, the vice president recruited me, took me under his wings and my career took off. Unfortunately, it was short-lived as my sponsor left for greener pastures at corporate headquarters.

## KEY POINTS

Get smart. Read everything you can about your organization, your industry and the key issues.

Keep your head down and work hard.

Identify not only the current leaders and power brokers, but the future ones as well. As the famous hockey player Wayne Gretzky once said when someone asked about the key to his success, "I don't skate where the puck is but rather where the puck's going to be."

Once you identify the key leaders in your organization, position yourself with them. Volunteer, send thank you notes, network, attend company functions, and be conversant with company financials and industry trends. Be physically and mentally fit, dress for success!

Just as importantly, avoid over lobbying or worse, being a "brown noser" and/or a self-promoter. Work the crowd but not at the expense of being perceived of doing it for the wrong reasons. Ideally, your sponsor will identify you and it will happen naturally. But if it doesn't, identify someone you feel could offer advice and coach you, and potentially serve as a strategic sponsor. But don't get too comfortable or rely too heavily on your sponsor, as they will not be around forever. And most importantly, when you make it, help others make it!

**"You can have everything in life you want, if you will just help enough other people get what they want."**
*Zig Ziglar*

## YOU REALLY SCREWED UP!

That was the text from my boss after I mishandled a big project. Lessons learned: Take the butt chewing, admit responsibility, avoid excuses, and make a list of lessons learned. Realize there are debits and credits to everyone's personal credibility and trust level. Depending on the severity of your screw up, it could take several deposits to get you out of credibility debt.

Keep your head up, plow ahead, and don't dwell on the past. Don't keep apologizing as that not only reminds others about the screw up, it can be annoying. Learn from your mistake and don't repeat. Just as with the recovery process in customer service, you may be able to create more loyalty and respect than before the screw up – it depends on your recovery.

**"If you're going to eat crow, eat it warm and eat it early!"**
*My Dad*

## QUESTIONS FOR CONSIDERATION

1. Why is understanding and appreciating organizational governance important?

2. How do organizations discriminate with levels/pay grades? What can/should be done to minimize this?

3. Describe the chain of command in your organization. What degree is it enforced and valued?

4. Where are you on the scale of lobbying for your needs and wants? Have you ever over lobbied? Under lobbied? Please describe.

5. How does someone get ahead in your organization?

6. What role do sponsors play in your organization?

## ADDITIONAL THOUGHTS

**Punctuality**. Arriving only five minutes early is five minutes late! If you're required to be at work at 8:00am and you regularly cruise in at 7:55am, you're not going to be on anyone's promotion list.

**Be Prepared**. Always show up to a meeting with pen and paper, and be prepared to discuss the topics on the agenda. Purchase a nice leather portfolio and look professional. Look/act/dress/perform one level above where you are, and where you want to be.

**Voice Mail/Email**. Your voice mail introduction should project a "Yes Face" and professional attitude. I continue to be surprised and perplexed by professionals who use a generic introduction or worse, none at all. Be careful of the perceived tone of your emails. You may mean nothing curt by a brief email message, but the one at the other end could perceive you as being abrupt or rude. A simple, "Thanks!" at the end of an email could make the difference. Avoid lengthy epistles when a short email or a text will suffice – pick up the phone if you have something important to discuss. Avoid leaving long voice mails.

**Drinking Alcohol**. Be very careful – more than one career has ended after the annual Christmas party. If you must, limit yourself to one-two drinks.

**Language/Grammar/Volume**. Swearing is something I have to be careful as my expressive personality occasionally feels the need to punctuate the conversation with some color. But it's best to simply avoid swearing.

Be cognizant of your grammar. Being from a rural background, this was an issue for me in college. While it stung, a college professor gave me valuable feedback when he said, "Greg, to reach the goals you've set for yourself, you're going to have to work on your grammar." He was right and I committed to improving my grammar, all the while modeling myself after others who were more polished than me. As far as volume, don't be the loudest in the room but don't be the "soft talker" where others have to strain to hear you. Remember, the key to success is balance and moderation.

**The Oxygen in the Room**. We've all been around that person who, when they walk into a room, immediately depletes the oxygen due to their constantly talking about themselves, always right, etc. Add fresh air by focusing on others rather than yourself, asking questions, being conversational. Commit to being a great listener!

**The Pie.** View success as an unlimited pie. Just because someone else succeeds doesn't decrease the likelihood of you getting a big slice too. Be happy for others. Jealousy will not only eat you alive, it will diminish career opportunities and relationships.

**Pull Others Up!** Are you helping people out of the bucket or pulling them down? "Crab Mentality" is a way of thinking best described by the phrase "If I can't have it, neither can you." The metaphor refers to a pot of crabs. Individually, the crabs could easily escape from the pot, but instead, they grab at each other in a useless "king of the hill" competition, which prevents any from escaping and ensures their collective demise. Don't be a crab!

**Be Conversant**. Expand your views and interests outside your immediate career and current position. Read at least one newspaper every day and keep up with current events and popular culture. Review industry websites on a regular basis. Pursue industry certifications, attend conferences, and subscribe to professional journals, on your dime if necessary.

**Networking**. Successful people build impressive networks. Always have a business card available at social events, send thank you notes as a follow up to meetings. Facilitate relationships, be that one person who coordinates breakfasts, lunches, dinners, after-hours get-togethers, Saturday morning golf or tennis, etc.

**Loyalty**. "Dance with the one that brung you." While a VP may notice your skills and talents, your immediate boss is the reason you're there. Be careful of headhunters recruiting you from the outside while you're on company time. If your boss ever perceives you as someone who is looking for another job and as someone who is not loyal, you may find yourself looking for employment out of necessity versus on your terms. Welcome and help that new person feel included.

**Make the Most of Your Time!** Imagine your bank crediting your account each morning with $86,400. However, every evening the bank deletes whatever part of the balance you failed to use during the day. What would you do? Draw out every cent, of course! Each of us has such a bank. Its name is Time. Every morning, it credits you with, 86,400 seconds. Every night it writes off as lost, whatever time you have failed to invest to a good purpose. It carries over no balance. It allows no overdraft.

Time opens a new account for you each day. Each night it burns the remains of the day. If you fail to use the day's deposits, the loss is yours. There's no drawing against "tomorrow." You must live in the present on today's deposits. Invest it to get the utmost in health, happiness and success. The clock is running. Make the most of your time.

**Memento Mori** (*Don't Get Too Big for Your Britches.*) In ancient Rome, victorious military leaders were paraded through the streets to be celebrated by the masses. Behind the general, in the same chariot, a soldier stood whose sole responsibility was to remind the general of his mortality, as a hedge against excessive pride (the kind that comes before the fall). "Memento Mori," the soldier would whisper, "Someday you will die." Even on the general's greatest day, the Romans included a mechanism by which the conqueror was reminded that he too would be on the receiving end of bad luck at some future date.

# Chapter 29

## Soft Skill Strategies

### BEING GOOD IN ADDITION TO BEING GREAT

"The Greatest Generation" was coined by journalist Tom Brokaw to describe the generation who grew up in the United States during the Great Depression and then went on to fight in World War II. Brokaw included those women and men whose productivity from the war's home front made a decisive and material contribution to the war effort. Brokaw wrote in his 1998 book *The Greatest Generation*, "It is, I believe, the greatest generation any society has ever produced." He argued that these men and women fought not for fame and recognition, but because it was the "right thing to do." No doubt this generation was "great," but what made them great was they were first "good."

It has been said that America is great because she is first good. In the bestseller *Good to Great*, the authors suggest that truly "great" companies were first "good" companies. The leaders of these "good to great" companies were not flashy and flamboyant. In fact, they were a lot like most World War II heroes: modest, simple, and salt of the earth.

I must admit I haven't had much interest in World War II, but after giving one of my keynote speeches, which included several military stories, a retired pilot approached me with tears in his eyes. He asked if I had heard a story about a German fighter pilot having sympathy for an American and his crew during a dogfight over war-torn Germany. In the story, rather than shoot down the American and his crew, the German pilot actually escorted the Americans out of harm's way pointing them safely toward England.

I had not heard that story before, but having two pretty powerful pilot stories in my first book and keynote speech, my new friend had certainly piqued my interest about the possibility of adding a third. To my surprise, the incident was the subject of a book, *A Higher Call: An Incredible True Story of Combat and Chivalry in the War-Torn Skies of World War II*, by Adam Mako.

As the story goes, the two pilots were American Charlie Brown and German Franz Stigler. The incident occurred on December 20, 1943, when after a successful bomb run on Germany, Charles 'Charlie' Brown's B-17 Flying Fortress was severely damaged by German fighters. Ace pilot Franz Stigler had an opportunity to shoot down the crippled U.S. bomber, but instead, for humanitarian reasons, he allowed the crew to fly back to their airfield in England. Stigler literally flew right over Brown's wing, safely escorting them until they reached the ocean, and departing with a salute to the American pilot.

Later, Stigler remembered the words of one of his commanding officers, "You are pilots. You don't score kills. You score victories. If I ever hear of you shooting at someone in a parachute, I'll shoot you myself." Stigler later commented, "To me, it was just like they were in a parachute. I saw them and they and their plane were so torn apart, I couldn't shoot them down."

Amazingly, Brown managed to fly the 250 miles across the ocean and safely land his severely damaged plane. After a flight debriefing to inform his officers about how a German pilot let him go, Brown was told not to repeat this to the rest of the unit so as to not build any positive sentiment toward enemy pilots.

Stigler said nothing of the incident to his commanding officers, knowing that a German pilot who spared the enemy while in combat risked execution. The two pilots actually met each other 40 years later, became close friends, and remained so until their deaths.

In the book, *Short of the Glory: The Fall and Redemption of Edward F. Prichard, Jr.*, the late Ed Prichard was quoted as saying, "Great men are seldom good men." Those words have both haunted and motivated me throughout my life. To some degree, we all fall into the category of "greatness." The late Prichard's advice is that we can't afford to let that greatness get in the way of being "good," a key Soft Skill.

In the brilliant movie *Saving Private Ryan*, an aging James Ryan returns with his family to the military cemetery in Normandy. He visits the grave of Captain John Miller, the man who, a half a century before, led the mission to save Private Ryan. At the end of the mission, Miller was fatally wounded. As he lay dying, Miller's final words to Private Ryan were, "James. Earn this . . . earn it."

We then see Ryan kneeling at Captain Miller's grave, marked by a white cross. Ryan, his voice trembling with emotion, says, "Every day I think about what you said to me that day on the bridge. I tried to live my life the best that I could. I hope that was enough. I hope that, at least in your eyes, I've earned what all of you have done for me." Weeping, Ryan turns to his wife and says, "Tell me I've led a good life...tell me I am a good man." Confused, she responds, "What?" Choked up, he manages to make a second request, "Tell me I'm a good man." Her response, like this entire scene, chokes me up even now: "You are."

## THANK THE UNSUNG HEROES

CEO of Charles Schwab, Walt Bettinger, tells the story of failing a test in business school. He said that it was one of his last college exams, which ruined his pristine 4.0 average, which taught him how important it was to recognize individuals "who do the real work."

After spending hours studying and memorizing formulas for calculations, he showed up to find that the exam was nothing but a blank sheet of paper. "The professor said, 'I've taught you everything I can teach you about business in the last 10 weeks," he recalled. "But the most important message, the most important question, is this: What's the name of the lady who cleans this building?"

He had no idea. He failed the exam and got a B in the class. "That had a powerful impact," he said. "Her name was Dottie, and I didn't know Dottie. I'd seen her, but I'd never taken the time to ask her name." Since then, he's "tried to know every Dottie I've worked with." "It was a great reminder of what really matters in life," he said.

John Wesley (1703-1791), one of the founders of the Methodist church, had a reputation of beginning work very early every day when he prayed, composed many of his great writings, and planned the beginnings of what is today one of the largest church denominations in the world. But John Wesley would later say the real hero was his personal assistant who arrived at his office a full hour before he did, started a fire and prepared hot tea for the morning.

In my workshops, I ask a simple question: "How many have a more than year-old note of appreciation that still remains in your desk or on your bulletin board?" Most raise their hand. In fact, numerous studies indicate the top reason for employee engagement is feeling appreciated. Consider leaving notes for the unsung heroes in your life that might say, "Thank you for all that you do! I appreciate and value you!"

## THINK, LAUGH AND
## HAVE YOUR EMOTIONS MOVED TO TEARS

Many of us can remember what has been called the greatest college basketball game of all time: the 1982 NCAA Championship game when North Carolina State upset the favored University of Houston team. (*Here's your homework assignment: Google YouTube of "NC State upsetting Houston Cougars, 1982."*) I will never forget Coach Jim Valvano running onto the court after that game, all his players already celebrating with other teammates, where he stood alone, desperately looking for someone to hug.

I remember the feeling of wanting to jump through the TV and hug an overwhelmed and excited Jim Valvano. That scene has never left me. In fact, it has provided the inspiration and my personal goal to be sincerely happy for other's success as I was for Jim Valvano at the end of that game in 1982.

*\* Who are the "Jim Valvanos" in your life who are running around life's court looking for someone to hug? It doesn't have to be a hug. A phone call or a note letting them know how happy you are for them or even how much they mean to you.*

Ten years after that game and only a few months before losing his battle to cancer, Jim Valvano received the Arthur Ashe Humanitarian Award (*Homework Assignment: Google YouTube of Jim Valvano accepting the Arthur Ashe Humanitarian Award*) and in front of thousands of supporters and millions of TV viewers, the wisdom of a dying man challenged us all to do three simple things every day. The following is an excerpt from that heart wrenching speech:

*To me, there are three things we all should do every day. We should do this every day of our lives. Number one is laugh. You should laugh every day. Number two is think. You should spend some time in thought. Number three is to have your emotions moved to tears. But think about it. If you laugh, you think, and you cry, that's a full day. That's a heck of a day. You do that seven days a week; you're going to have something special."*

I don't think Jim Valvano meant a "boo hoo" cry as much as he meant what I experienced a few years ago when I got a little emotional—a little choked up—when I witnessed a friend of mine's adult autistic son jump into his arms and exclaim, "I love you dad!"

Or maybe when I was at an intersection and see approximately ten young ladies with posters that read, "Free Hugs." I then see two mechanics running out of a service station and getting a hug from each one of these young ladies. I was moved to tears. Later, I found out these young ladies represented an army of roughly 10,000 Paul Mitchell Salon students who take to the street every September 23rd throughout the United States and celebrate their nationwide "Free Hugs Day."

And as I moved my car to the next intersection I see ten more of these young ladies. I blew my horn and they waved and screamed. I quickly put my car in park, opened my door, and received ten of the sweetest, warmest and most sincere hugs in the world! Again, I was moved to tears. I thought, Jimmy V would be proud! Little did I know my own daughter would eventually attend a Paul Mitchell school and participate in the "Free Hugs Day!"

"As members of the beauty industry, we're in the business of helping people look beautiful. More importantly, it's part of our 'Be Nice' culture to help people feel beautiful. Our Free Hugs campaign is just one of the many ways our future professionals show their passion and compassion in their local communities," says Winn Claybaugh, Dean and Cofounder of Paul Mitchell Schools.

## TELLING SOMEONE OFF:
## SHORT-TERM IMPACT; PERMANENT DAMAGE

My teenage daughter worked at a local diner and would come into our bedroom upon returning from what were usually very long nights, aching feet, and not much to show in the form of wages for her labor. While most conversations consisted of, "I'm tired, going to bed, love you all," one visit was significantly more dramatic. She entered our bedroom in tears.

She told the story of an irate customer who was less than pleasant. Not only did the angry customer scream, yell and use foul language, she called the owner on the way home and insisted he fire my daughter. Needless to say, she was very upset. Naturally, this led to my wife and me getting upset as well. Our anger intensified and concern for our daughter's emotional state grew.

And while it's never a good idea to "tell someone off," we've all probably been guilty of crossing the "Soft Skills" line. But while we're "giving it to them," making our point, there's someone's day we've just ruined. Maybe even ruining their night, their weekend. Additionally, we've negatively impacted families, assuming they share their hurt feelings with others as my daughter did with my wife and me after her encounter.

We're not talking about delivering constructive feedback to a service provider regarding expectations not met, services not delivered. We're talking about losing our composure, creating a scene and damaging someone's self-esteem. And it's not just service providers we should avoid "telling off." It's that person in our office, a friend, a colleague, and a family member. What might seem completely justified could be devastating to that person.

It's not just the tone and volume of one's voice. The words we use can be equally if not more damaging. A Sunday school teacher made the point of how damaging our words can be to another person. She distributed a small piece of wood, a nail and hammer instructing each student to hammer a nail into each piece of wood. The nail represented a word(s) that may have hurt someone. The hammer was then used to remove the nail representing the forgiveness one sought. But even if the apology is accepted, the hole in the piece of wood remains representing the memory of the hurt.

"Telling someone off" is not only a bad idea, it rarely delivers the desired results. I remember witnessing an airline gate agent getting an earful from an angry passenger. The unruly passenger ranted and raved, he huffed and puffed and used profanity. The gate agent kept her composure, responded in a professional manner and eventually managed to get the passenger on another flight. After the angry passenger moved on, the passenger in front of me approached the counter and immediately complimented the gate agent on her cool, calm and collected demeanor in dealing with the previous customer.

Her response, "Thank you for that feedback. That gentleman is going to Denver, his bags are going to Detroit!"

## SOFT SKILLS OBSERVATIONS FROM A SUMMER VACATION

Vacation is a time to relax, unwind and reconnect with family and friends. But it can also be a time for reflection. On a recent vacation, I jotted down 15 observations that have become much clearer as I've gotten older. I hope you enjoy the list and that it provides a source of reflection on your next vacation.

1. **The beauty and diversity of people**. As I walked the beach I not only saw some pretty interesting people, I noticed how beautiful the human race really is. Young people, middle aged people and very old people holding hands, laughing and simply enjoying life. We all have the same basic need to be happy.

2. **The importance of family**. As beautiful as the location might be, it's not the same without family to enjoy it. We've all attended conferences or meetings at exotic locations without our family and it just wasn't the same. Vacations provide a wonderful opportunity to spend quality time with family. Even if it's a simple trip to a water park just a few hours down the road, or the roadside parks of yesterday, the experience and memories are priceless!

3. **The chance to be a kid again**. On a recent vacation, we rented bikes and my wife and I rode for hours. We played in the sand, splashed in the water and took long walks. Unfortunately, my grandparents were old at 50. My wife's Uncle Jim was the complete opposite. Jim vowed to water ski every year until he died. I can still see him wobbling up on two water skis, white hair waving in the wind. He would ski for a few minutes, let go of the rope and sink in the water on his terms. Be Jim!

4. **The richness of local history, sites, attractions**. Just taking time to read the back of the menu at your favorite vacation restaurant can be a lesson in vision, purpose, perseverance, entrepreneurism and following one's dreams.

5. **The opportunity to "sharpen the saw."** Vacations are wonderful opportunities to recharge your batteries. Try to leave work at home and enjoy yourself.

6. **It's all about the memories**. Disney World has it right when they say they're in the memory creation business. Most likely your kids won't remember where you went on vacation as much as the family simply being together for an entire week with your undivided attention. Remember to "Be Here Now."

7. **Don't forget while you're on vacation, others are working**. As my wife and I rode our bikes one morning, I couldn't help but notice all the people responsible for keeping our vacation spot pristine. The waitresses and waiters who busted their buns in making sure my family and I were having a good meal deserved a pat on the back. I'm ashamed that I didn't thank them enough. More than a good tip, actually pulling that waitress aside and say, "Thank you for creating a beautiful memory for my family and me tonight!"

8. **Everyone's friendly on vacation**. Why can't we take that positive attitude, those Soft Skills, back home with us and exhibit it every day? I'm going to try!

9. **The need to be extra careful**. We're not as young as we used to be. Falls hurt more and last longer. A friend of ours had a nasty bike wreck on vacation and is still recuperating. Sunburns can make a vacation miserable, especially on the first day!

10. **Reflect and plan for the future**. I find I'm a little more ambitious, more of a dreamer while on vacation. This might be the perfect opportunity to set goals for the future and commit to start that business or take that risk you've been contemplating. Explore the "Potential!"

11. **Simplicity**. That small space my family and I stay while on vacation is always enough space to live comfortably. These realizations reinforce the need and importance to simplify, to downsize.

12. **Be-Here-Now**. The importance of living in the present. Not thinking of having to leave on Saturday while your family is enjoying the beach on Tuesday. Giving your family undivided attention and being that happy person when you return like you were on vacation.

13. **Naps**. Vacations are wonderful opportunities to get caught up on sleep. Some cultures actually take naps every day. It works for them, maybe it could for us!

14. **Ice Cream**. I'm convinced world peace could be achieved if factions would simply stop fighting and have an ice cream cone together. A friend of mine tells the story of his boss taking everyone in the office out for ice cream a few times a year. The McDonalds in my hometown sends ice cream to the local nursing home on a regular basis. The employees and residents go crazy!

15. **Last but certainly not least, seeing first-hand the wonders of God**. The ocean, the mountains, the beauty of the outdoors. Your family, the love you share, laughter, happiness, sunrises and sunsets. As the late Louis Armstrong sang so beautifully, "What a Wonderful World!"

Enjoy your next vacation!

## HOW'S THE VIEW?

We moved my mother into a rehab facility after double knee replacement. She shared a room with Ms. Wilson who had a window view and described the beautiful scenery most of the afternoon. Ms. Wilson was scheduled to leave in a few days and commented to my mother that it would better for her to get the "window side" of the room upon her departure.

This exchange reminded me of two elderly men in a VA hospital and in a similar situation. One was by the window and one by the wall. Depressed, the gentleman by the wall asks his roommate to describe the view out the window. Each day the gentleman by the window describes the following, "I see children playing, I see birds flying, and I see couples holding hands."

The gentleman by the wall responds, "Tell me more." The man by the window continues, "It's an absolutely beautiful day. Leaves are falling, looks like a nice breeze and a father and son are flying a kite." This continues for weeks until the gentleman by the window passes away. His roommate moves to the window side of the room. As he looks out the window anticipating seeing what his friend had been describing for weeks, he sees nothing but a solid brick wall.

I think of how many times I had the chance to paint a picture of children playing, of birds flying, of couples holding hands and instead painted a picture of a solid brick wall. For many, we may be the only hope and inspiration with whom they come in contact. They see "Bricks" while we see "Cathedrals." Share the view!

## NO HITS, NO RUNS, NO ERRORS

An elderly woman dies in a small community. She was a simple woman, lived a simple life outliving most relatives and friends. When she died the local newspaper attempted to write her obituary. While the editor had known of the women nothing really stood out as noteworthy to mention in her obituary. Frustrated, he delegated the task to his junior editor. She found herself in the same predicament and passed the assignment to other associates where it eventually landed on the sports editor's desk. The following week the elderly women's obituary read,

"No Hits, No Runs, No Errors."

This lady could have been any of our grandmothers who may not have been known for contributing anything particularly newsworthy. But like my grandmother and probably yours, she supported, developed and nurtured greatness behind the scenes

everyday of her life. The above story and many like it prompt me to question my own contributions. Specifically, what is my purpose? What drives my behavior? Where am I spending my time, my energy and where is my focus? What legacy do I want to leave?

I'm reminded of a story where Apple's Steve Jobs was recruiting John Sculley, vice-president at PepsiCo. Sculley had successfully made Pepsi the number one brand in the Cola Wars. There was really no reason for him, one of America's top managers with a secure and highly paid position, to join a bunch of young computer nerds at Apple. Sculley finally agreed to join Apple because of a question Jobs asked him: "Do you want to spend the rest of your life selling colored sugared water or do you want a chance to change the world?" Sculley left PepsiCo.

In Bob Buford's best-selling book, *Half Time*, he uses the metaphor of a football game. He suggests we don't think too much about the contributions we've made in the "first half" of our lives. We rush through school, get married, start a career, climb the company ladder, and buy lots of toys. At some point in our lives however we start to wonder if this is as good as it gets? Somehow, keeping score doesn't offer the thrill it once did. During the first half, we may have taken some vicious hits and suffered personal setbacks.

While we start the "second half" with good intentions, we get blindsided along the way. While the first half was about success, the second half should be about significance, about making a difference. The game is won or lost in the second half, not the first. Some people never get to the second half, as the prevailing view in our society is that once you reach your fifties, you enter a period of aging and decline. Like Buford, I challenge you to discredit the view that the second half of our lives will never measure up to the first and change the focus from success to significance.

What contributions are you making? Are you seeking significance over success? How would you define your purpose? And as morbid as it might sound, how would your epitaph read? I hope mine reads something like this, "Several hits and runs, a few errors with the batter going down swinging!" Or maybe steal a classic line from a Jimmy Buffett song (Growing Older But Not Up), "I would rather die while I'm living than live while I'm dead."

## AN ENCOURAGER

In the Solomon Islands in the south Pacific villagers practice a unique form of logging. If a tree is too large to be cut with an ax, the natives cut it down by yelling at it. Woodsmen creep up on a tree just at dawn and suddenly scream at it at the top of their lungs. They continue this for thirty days and legend has it, the tree dies and falls over. The theory is that the yelling kills the spirit of the tree.

Sound crazy? Yes, but we participate in a similar and equally damaging practice of "screaming" at others (children, employees, spouses, significant others) and killing their spirit. The words we use, the tone in which we respond can having a chilling effect on others. And even silence and/or ignoring someone can kill their spirit!

A friend of mind played college football at a Top 10 school with most of his team going on to play at the professional level. In his opinion, the one that had the most talent simply disappeared after one of his best collegiate games. After a game where this gifted athlete scored numerous touchdowns and was responsible for many game-changing plays, the coach felt it necessary to make sure this player didn't get "too full of himself."

A derogatory remark by the coach made what should have been the best day in this athlete's life into the reason for him quitting the team, and eventually checking out of life. In telling this story, my friend recalled, "I remember that day like it was yesterday. I remember the coach's remark to my teammate as he ran off the field, seeing him go from total elation to total rejection."

Many years later, my friend and his college teammates were planning a reunion and set out to find all the players. Guess who they couldn't find? You're right, the teammate that had been rejected by the coach that day. They eventually found their long-lost friend but it was too late. He had passed away just a few months before they visited their late friend's son. After explaining the reason for their quest, the son commented that he never knew his father had even played college ball. Sadly, that irresponsible coach killed our friend's spirit, and destroyed his memory and legacy of playing for one of the nation's powerhouse college football programs.

In a recent sermon, our minister's message was, "The ministry of Encouragement." He spoke of Barnabas and how he encouraged John Mark and the difference of opinion between him (Barnabas) and Paul. Paul didn't want John Mark to accompany them on their second campaign. Barnabas didn't give up, which cost him the relationship with Paul. Barnabas' support and encouragement of John Mark is why we have the book of Mark.

We're all in the ministry of Encouragement. At work, at home, with our friends, with co-workers, with family. Maybe a simple phone call, a note could make all the difference in the world. Do we stand up for the "John Marks" in our lives? Do we encourage or "yell at the tree?" Do we hurt others with our words? Be an Encourager!

## LEARNING FROM A WILDCAT

Whether you're a Kentucky Wildcat fan or not, few would argue with the amazing demonstration of talent and athleticism Coach John Calipari manages to put together year after year. I've always admired Calipari not so much for his coaching ability and the teams he assembles year after year but for his leadership abilities, how he treats others and his seeming mastery of the Soft Skills. The following are a few examples:

- **The Words We Use**. Calipari doesn't use the word, "substitutions," for those players who don't start, he uses, "reinforcements." Sure it might just be semantics but the words we use are very important. Calipari's success in recruiting often results in having too much talent. That's where the idea to "platoon" with two separate five-man units was born. Not "subs," but "reinforcements." Not "second string," but "platoons."

## KEY QUESTION

1. How careful are we with the words we use? With family members? With team members? With each other? A friend of mine reminds me that one "Aw crap" erases ten "Atta boys!"

- **Calipari helps his team see the "Big Picture."** It's almost a given that most of Calipari's players will have the opportunity to make money playing basketball when they leave UK. They may not start or even play an entire game, but they will have a bright future if they play as a team and are committed to the "Big Picture."

2. How good of a job do we do in reminding our team of the "Big Picture?"

3. Does that "Big Picture" inspire excellence? Are they committed?

- **Calipari is a Level 5 Leader**. In Jim Collins best-selling book, *Good to Great*, he describes a Level 5 leader as someone who builds enduring greatness through a paradoxical blend of personal humility and professional will. A Level 5 leader has an ego, but the ego is about the organization and not about them. After winning the National Championship in 2012, Calipari said, "It's not about me. It's not about the one who plays the entire game. It's about that young man who didn't get much playing time this year, could have been playing every second at most Division 1 schools in the Country but would rather be here instead. That's who this is about."

4. Is our ego more about the organization or about us?

5. How good of a job do we do in thanking all the members of our team and not just the superstars?

- **Managing Expectations and Keeping Egos in Check**: After a recent romp, the Wildcats played a scrappy team and struggled. They won but it wasn't the same performance. Calipari commented, "Our players are not robots, they're kids. We're not going to play every game at that level."

• **Speaking Favorably of the Competition**. This is something business could learn from sports. I have respect for someone who says, "They're a good company, I can see why you use them. I would be honored if the opportunity ever presents itself you would consider using us," versus downgrading the competition. Calipari and his opponents almost always praise the opposing team. After a Boston University game, Coach Joe Jones said, "I've never seen a team that deep and that long. You guys are going to have a lot of fun nights."

6. How often have we praised our competition?
7. Have we been guilty of downgrading our competition for no particular reason? In today's business climate today's competition could be tomorrow's partner.

• **Make Needed Corrections**. Almost every game, whether Kentucky or another team, the team that plays the second half is not the same team that played the first half. They make the needed corrections and in most cases are a far more effective team. Even on the sidelines (and unlike most coaches), Calipari disciplines with compassion versus demeaning a player with screaming and cursing.

8.  Do we pause to ask what we need to do differently to achieve true greatness in the "Second Half" of our lives?
9.  Do we discipline with compassion?

- **IQ in addition to EI (Emotional Intelligence.)** Calipari is no doubt a genius on the court. But he's also the epitome of Emotional Intelligence. He naturally connects with others in a deep and visceral way. His players love him. His fans love him. He lights up a room and a gymnasium when he enters. People naturally want to be around him.

10. Your IQ is high but what about your EQ?

- **Complacency Management.** After the Wildcats beat a local state team in its first exhibition game, that coach was asked to identify a possible UK weakness. He offered this word of caution. "I think there will be times when they have to avoid getting fat-and-happy. They have to stay hungry all the time and all night."

Using a metaphor of a rubber band between two index fingers, Peter Senge in his book *The Fifth Discipline*, suggests we create and maintain "Creative Tension" with our teams. Too loose and we're bored. Too stretched and we're about to pop. With a healthy tension we're at our best. Many athletes call this state-of-mind "Flow."

11. How are we doing creating and maintaining "Creative Tension" with our teams?
12. Are they bored, challenged or on the verge of a breakdown?

- **Empower Your Team.** During a post-game interview, Calipari commented on one of his players showing signs of fatigue during the second half. He immediately shared the conversation with the "platoon" that weren't on the floor. Calipari told his team, "If you notice one of your teammates wearing down don't wait for me to put you in, put yourself in!"

13. Are you empowering your teams or are they waiting for you to make all the decisions?

- **Wearing the 100-Pound Coat.** Calipari describes the pressure of playing for Kentucky like wearing a 100-pound coat while your competition is wearing a nylon windbreaker. Each opponent prepares and plays Kentucky like it's a Final Four game. Calipari tells recruits if you can't take that kind of pressure than Kentucky is not for you.

14. How well do you handle the competitive pressure coming at you every day?
15. Do we prepare our teams for that kind of pressure?

No one knows what this season holds for the Kentucky Wildcats or for that matter, what the upcoming season holds for any of us. When I consider making predictions, I think of my friend, the late David Garvin, founder of Camping World. Every year, he would make the following eight predictions:

(1) Business will continue to go where invited and remain where appreciated.
(2) Reputations will continue to be made by many acts and lost by only one.
(3) People will continue to prefer doing business with friends.
(4) Performance will continue to outsell promises.
(5) Enthusiasm will be as contagious as ever.

(6)  Know-how will surpass guess-how.

(7)  Trust, not tricks, will keep customers loyal.

(8)  The extra mile will have no traffic jams.

Simple yet profound.

## THE POWER OF TOUCH

My grandmother was a resident of a nursing home and one day after a visit I found myself having difficulty finding my way to the exit. As I turned the corner, visibly confused and disoriented, a young orderly took notice and came to my rescue. Frustrated, I asked, "Can you help me get out of here?"

"Walk with me," the young man said as he guided me through the labyrinth of hallways and corridors. Not, "Go down that hallway, take a left, a right then another left." As we navigated our way to the closest exit, numerous patients suffering from dementia were lined in the hallways, sitting in their wheelchairs unresponsive, heads down and completely unaware of our journey past them.

With the precision of a skilled surgeon, this young man placed his tender and loving hand on the shoulder of each patient he passed – creating a visible reaction in each person he touched. It was as if each patient he touched asked, "Who touched me?" This young man, who may have never attended a seminar or read a book on the power of touch, provided a dose of medicine more effective than any conventional treatment. He did this naturally, with love and compassion.

I am reminded of Luke 8: 44-46 where the woman touches the garment of Jesus. "Who was it that touched me?" Jesus asks. Peter responds, "There are many people around you." Jesus continues, "Someone touched me, for I perceive the power has gone out of me." Just like the orderly at the nursing home, we too have the power to touch others when it originates from the heart, when it's sincere and full of love.

## HELP OTHERS REALIZE WHAT THEY DO MAKES A DIFFERENCE

My son worked at McDonalds during high school and occasionally I would stop on my way to work to say hello. One morning while leaving that McDonald's parking lot, I saw a gentleman sweeping and picking up trash. Obviously, he didn't look too excited. As I passed, I rolled down my window and said, "I want to tell you how great this parking lot looks! My first impression of a restaurant is how clean the parking lot is and you're doing an excellent job!"

Initially stunned but eventually smiling, he said, "Thank you." I can still remember looking in the rearview mirror and noticing the "pep in his step" as he continued cleaning the parking lot. That night my son asked, "Did you tell Scott how good the parking lot looked this morning?" When I answered in the affirmative, my son replied, "You made his day!"

A former boss of mine used to call each direct report on Christmas Eve and simply tell each of us how much we meant to him, what a difference we were making for the company, and in general how much he appreciated our friendship and commitment to the company. Naturally, I would have done anything for this man. It was the difference between "commitment" and "compliance."

Managers seek compliance; leaders receive commitment. It was a simple but very powerful gesture that created a culture of appreciation, and paid both financial and emotional dividends. Interestingly, after that boss left our division for a promotion at corporate, my wife exclaimed, "I miss John like a death!" Think about it. An inspirational leader who gave a personal touch that not only motivated the employee, but also garnered the support and admiration of the employee's spouse! Very powerful.

## THE POWER OF A NOTE

Some credit Jimmy Carter's successful run for governor of Georgia to his handwritten notes to everyone he met on the campaign trail. When he was campaigning, a staff member would follow behind the candidate and say to every person he met, "You just met Jimmy Carter and we think he's going to be the next governor of Georgia. We'd like to send you some information. Do you mind giving us your name and address?" The staff person would get the name of the entire family.

Each person received a handwritten note – "Dear Joel and Pam, you just met Jimmy Carter, hopefully the next governor of Georgia. We would appreciate your vote, so nice to see you, thank you very much." Signed: Jimmy Carter. A real signature, not an electronic one!

Handwritten notes make a real difference in creating brand loyalty, and cost very little money. I travel on a regular basis and have stayed in almost every hotel chain across the country, each hoping to create some level of loyalty in the process. In most rooms there's a standard feedback form asking a series of questions related to my stay. Were you satisfied with the check-in process? Were you satisfied with the cleanliness of your room? Quality of food? Amenities of the hotel? I rarely take the time to complete those.

However, on a business trip to Missouri, I stayed at a Holiday Inn Express and was blown away as I checked into my third floor room. I had been on the road all week, missing my family and exhausted from the day's work. As I opened the door, threw my suitcase on the bed, and made my way to the nightstand to plug my cell phone charger into the wall outlet, I noticed what looked like a small inexpensive thank you card. As I opened the card I was blown away with not only the simplicity of this customer service gesture, but the sincerity that went into writing it.

> Hello!
>
> Thank you for taking the time to read this card. As your housekeepers, we would like to welcome you to the 3rd floor. It is our goal to make sure your experience is a happy and relaxing time. We want you to think of this room as your home away from home, not just another hotel room. If there is anything we can do to improve your stay, please let us know. Thank you for choosing the Holiday Inn Express.
>
> Enjoy your stay,
>
> Trudy & Michelle

Which hotel created loyalty? The glitzy four-star hotel with the generic feedback form printed on the finest card stock or the Holiday Inn Express that empowered their house cleaning staff to make guests feel as comfortable as possible and find some personal and unique way to thank customers for their business?

I was on the board of a non-profit organization where we sent thousands of letters requesting financial support. While the letter was a formal typed letter, each board member selected those with whom they had a personal connection and simply wrote a few lines to the right of the margin making an otherwise formal, very impersonal letter significantly more personal. For instance, a letter addressed to Jim had a few handwritten lines that would say something like this: "Jim, thanks for all that you do and the leadership you provide our community. Thanks in advance for your support!" It was then signed on the margin by the one who had the relationship. Instead of a formal letter with a stamped signature from an unknown person, it was from a friend with whom it would be hard not to provide some amount of support. Writer's cramp after signing 1,000 letters? Yes! Worth it? Yes, we doubled our fundraising goal!

## EVERYONE NEEDS A PRESENT; EVERYONE NEEDS ATTENTION

One year I was asked to play Santa Claus for the residents at a nursing home. I agreed, not really knowing what to expect, as my previous experiences had been with young children. The set up was basically the same with the exception of the roles being reversed. Instead of the parents bringing the children to see Santa Claus, the residents' families (usually their children) facilitated the visit and gifts from Santa Claus. I realize we leave this world the same way we enter, having someone take care of us and attending to our basic needs; however, I wasn't ready for what I was about to experience playing Santa Claus for the elderly.

The residents were as excited as young children with many usually nonresponsive patients suddenly coming alive when Santa Claus arrived. For most residents, it was as if Santa was an old friend they felt they should know but weren't quite sure who he was. And I responded as such. It wasn't the normal "Ho, Ho, Ho, Merry Christmas!" It was more like, "Hey, how in the world have you been?"

Unfortunately, nursing homes are not just for the elderly. In one room was a young man who was in the final stages of a deteriorating disease and while he could see, he was almost 100 percent immobile and unresponsive. While Santa Claus loved on this young man, I couldn't help but notice his parents crying, as they remembered happier holidays when their son was home and well.

As Santa Claus wandered into the main living room area, I started handing out the presents family members had brought for the residents. A few elves (nurses) that knew the residents' names would whisper, "This one is for Mr. Cornwell, he's sitting over there." I loved on every resident and the warmth I felt was indeed a spiritual experience. As I was handing out the presents, I felt a tug on Santa Claus's coat. It was an elderly lady who looked up at me with childlike eyes and sadly asked, "Where's my present?"

She was the only resident who did not have a gift and no relatives present for this holiday celebration. And while the employees hustled and finally found her a token present, the wait had been a painful one for both of us. The reality of what she must have felt while everyone else had stacks of presents continues to choke me up. We never get too old or too important for attention. And, we never outgrow the need for a present.

*"For I was hungry and you gave me something to eat, I was thirsty and you gave me something to drink, I was a stranger and you invited me in, I needed clothes and you clothed me, I was sick and you looked after me, I was in prison and you came to visit me.' Then the righteous will answer him, 'Lord, when did we see you hungry and feed you, or thirsty and give you something*

*to drink? When did we see you a stranger and invite you in, or needing clothes and clothe you? When did we see you sick or in prison and go to visit you?' The King will reply, 'Truly I tell you, whatever you did for one of the least of these brothers and sisters of mine, you did for me.'"*

Matthew 25: 35-40

## EVERYONE HAS A STORY TO TELL

I was in Washington DC at the Hyatt Regency Hotel attending a conference when I saw a shoeshine stand. One of life's greatest pleasures, in my opinion, is getting your shoes shined by a true professional. It is indeed a lost art. The sign at this particular shoeshine stand said, "Be back in 15 minutes." I had some free time so I waited. Within a few minutes, a very professional-looking man entered a small area near the men's restroom, removed his overcoat and asked, "Are you ready for a shoeshine sir?" A little surprised, I jumped up on the chair and let the man who looked like a United States Senator perform his magic.

I could have let this gentleman shine my shoes while I read my *USA Today*, paid the $6, and gone about my day. I would have missed an opportunity to be inspired and motivated by this man's story. I couldn't resist asking, "Would you tell me your story?" He told the story of growing up in New York and starting to shine shoes as a teenager at the local airport. He was recruited by the FBI, and later moved to Washington DC.

He continued moonlighting and shining shoes on the side, where he touched and inspired some of the most important and powerful people in the world. He eventually left the FBI and continues to shine shoes today, demonstrating how "Cathedrals" indeed come in many shapes and many forms. Everyone has a story to tell and for the most part, most want to be asked and take great pride and joy in telling their story. Don't miss the opportunity to inspire others, to learn from others, to sharpen your listening skills, to show the deepest respect ever, by simply asking others to tell you their story. And, be open to and not afraid to tell others your story!

## WORK HORSES; SHOW HORSES

When my father died he passed down his 1999 GMC truck to me. My dad was a simple and practical man who would give anyone the shirt off his back. He took care of others but didn't always take care of himself or in this case, his truck. Excited, I set out to clean my dad's truck. New bed liner, paint job and four new tires. Commenting to my wife the only thing left to do now was to wash the seats because of the smell. She asked, "What do they smell like?" My reply, "Dad." Specifically, the smell was an oily/paint smell as my dad spent his retirement as a handy man. In short, the truck smelled of "hard work." No doubt, my dad was the epitome of a workhorse!

Growing up, dad would take me to the bank on Friday afternoons where he would deposit the majority of his check from the local factory where he worked. While dad's outfit could be described as basic work clothes, the local bank president, Mr. Ashlock, wore a classic business suit. It was at this point I wanted a job where I could dress up every day. While Mr. Ashlock was a very hard worker and even farmed on the side, to me he was my first glimpse of a show horse.

But like most things, one needs to strike a balance. It's important to look the part but one has to play the part as well. I remember in graduate school having a cohort who was a pretty sharp fellow, at least in my eyes. He was a good-looking guy, dressed well and even moonlighted as a local TV personality. But every semester, he scrambled around the last week or so trying to complete past assignments, begging professors for extra credit to boost his past failures, etc. One professor with whom I had developed a close relationship commented about my associate one day. "He's a 357 Magnum shooting blanks!" Translation: Big Hat; No Cattle.

While I'm not too sure of the research on the correlation between how one feels and how one looks, I'm convinced it's out there! I'm reminded of a story Majority Floor Leader Rocky Adkins, one of the hardest working and most professional looking members of the Kentucky General Assembly, tells about his father who was a high school basketball coach. Coach Adkins didn't need research to make the connection between appearance and performance. On the court, Rep. Adkins recalls his father making sure his player's shoes were clean, socks pulled up and jerseys tucked in. Good sportsmanship was expected and anything less than a professional appearance would not be tolerated. Traveling to away games, Coach Adkins' team wore pressed slacks, matching sweaters, white button down shirts and polished shoes. In the words of Coach Adkins, "You play like you look."

## PREVAILING IN THE END

In my book, keynote speeches and leadership workshops, I introduce a metaphor of a "Fire" to describe personal and organizational setbacks we've all experienced. The metaphor originates from the fire of 1666 that leveled London. Pre 1666, London was a medieval town where 10,000 people annually died of the plague. The major cause of the plague was disease carrying rats and fleas. After the fire, the rats and fleas were eradicated. The leaders of London were determined to rebuild and make London a modern city. We too, like London, can emerge from both personal and organizational "fires" better, stronger, faster.

And while optimism played a big part in the leaders of London as they began to rebuild, I'm equally sure realistic expectations and a good dose of current reality played a part as well. The challenge is to *never confuse faith that we will prevail in the end—which we cannot afford to lose—with the discipline to confront the most brutal facts of our current reality (our "fires"), whatever they might be.*

This lesson is best explained in an interview with Admiral Jim Stockdale, who was the highest-ranking United States military officer in the "Hanoi Hilton" prisoner-of-war camp during the height of the Vietnam War. Tortured over 20 times during his eight-year imprisonment from 1965 to 1973, Stockdale lived out the war without any prisoner's rights, no set release date and no certainty as to whether he would ever see his family again. He shouldered the burden of command; doing everything he could to create conditions that would increase the number of prisoners who would survive unbroken, while fighting an internal war against his captors.

During the interview, Admiral Stockdale was asked what helped him and the other survivors endure the torture and isolation. He described elaborate communications systems, strategies to reduce the sense of isolation and even coping mechanisms they used while being tortured. Reluctantly, the interviewer finally asked the question, "Who didn't make it out?"

"Oh that's easy," he said. "The optimists." He continued, "The optimists. Oh, they were the ones who said, 'We're going to be out by Christmas.' And Christmas would come, and Christmas would go. Then they would say, 'We're going to be out by Easter.' And Easter would come, and Easter would go. And then Thanksgiving, and then it would be Christmas again. And they died of a broken heart." Stockdale then turned to the interviewer and said, "***This is a very important lesson. You must never confuse faith that you will prevail in the end—which you cannot afford to lose—with the discipline to confront the most brutal facts of your current reality, whatever they might be.***"

We all experience personal and organizational "fires," disappointments and setbacks for which there is no reason, no one to blame. Some "Fires" last longer than others. Some fires (the death of a loved one) we never get over. It may be losing a job or closing a business. It could be getting a divorce, recovering from an injury or losing an election. What separates those who come out of the "fires of life" from those who are forever burned is not the presence or absence of "fires," but how we deal with the inevitable difficulties of life. Keep pursuing your dreams but with the discipline to confront the "fires" of life. We will prevail in the end!

"At some point, everything's gonna go south on you... everything's going to go south and you're going to say, this is it.

SOFT SKILLS FIELD MANUAL

This is how I end. Now you can either accept that, or you can get to work. That's all it is. You just begin. You do the math. You solve one problem... and you solve the next one... and then the next. And if you solve enough problems, you get to come home."

~Astronaut Mark Watney character, played by Matt Damon, in the movie, "Martian."

## PACKING PARACHUTES

A friend of mine tells the story of a US Navy sailor he accidentally met several years after that sailor had actually saved his life. He was sitting in a restaurant in Kansas City and noticed a man about two tables away looking over at him. My friend didn't recognize him. A few minutes into his meal the sailor stood up, walked over to my friend's table, looked down at him, pointed his finger in his face and said, "You're Captain Plumb."

My friend looked up and said, "Yes, I'm Captain Plumb."

The sailor said, "You flew jet fighters in Vietnam. You were on the aircraft carrier Kitty Hawk. You were shot down. You parachuted into enemy hands and spent six years as a prisoner of war."

My friend said, "How in the world did you know all that?"

The sailor replied, "Because, I packed your parachute!"

My friend, Captain Charles Plumb USNR, (Ret.), is the author of "I'm No Hero: A POW Story" and travels the world telling this powerful story. Capt. Plumb and I have talked about that incident; he told me, "Greg, after that encounter, I was speechless. I staggered to my feet and held out a very grateful hand of thanks. This guy came up with the perfect response. He grabbed my hand and said, 'I guess it worked!'"

"Indeed it did, my friend," I said. "And I must tell you, I've said many prayers of thanks for your nimble fingers, but I never thought I'd have the opportunity to express my gratitude in person."

He asked, "Were all the panels there?"

"Well," I said, "I must be honest—of the 18 panels in that parachute, I had 15 good ones. Three were torn, but it wasn't your fault, it was mine. I jumped out of that jet fighter at a high rate of speed, and very close to the ground. That's what tore the panels in the chute. It wasn't the way you packed it."

"Now, let me ask you a question," I said. "Do you keep track of all the parachutes you've packed?" [Now what follows is perhaps the most significant part of the story.]

"No," he responded. "It's enough gratification for me just to know that I've served," responded the man who packed my parachute.

Capt. Plumb continued, "Greg, I didn't get much sleep that night. I kept thinking about that man. I kept wondering what he might have looked like in a Navy uniform; bib in the back, bell-bottom trousers, and a Dixie-cup hat. I wondered how many times I might have passed him on board the Kitty Hawk. I wondered how many times I might have seen him and not even said "Good morning," or "How are you?" or anything. You see, I was a fighter pilot and he was just a sailor. But how many hours did that sailor spend at that long wooden table in the bowels of that ship weaving the shrouds and folding the silks of those life-saving parachutes? I'm ashamed to admit that at the time, I could have cared less--until one day my parachute came along and he packed it for me!"

Charlie Plumb asked me some very thought provoking questions that I will pass along to you as the excerpt of our conversation continues:

"How's your "parachute packing" coming along? Who looks to you for strength in times of need? And perhaps, more importantly, who are the special people in your life who provide the encouragement you need when the chips are down?"

Capt. Plumb continued, "Perhaps it's time right now to give those people a call and thank them for packing your parachute. I needed a variety of 'parachutes' when my plane was shot down over enemy territory--I needed a physical parachute, a mental parachute, an emotional parachute, and most importantly, a spiritual parachute."

"I'm often asked: 'How did you do it, Commander? How did you survive six years in a prisoner of war camp? I could have never done it.' My answer is always, 'Of course you could.' My secret for enduring six years of hell is really not a secret at all. First and foremost, I had faith in an omniscient God, knowing that His will would be done. I never doubted that I could persevere; I simply trusted God's promise to answer my prayers. I also loved my country, its people, and its freedoms. I realized that, because of the human element, mistakes could be made. But in growing up I had discerned that most of the people in this great land are honorable and compassionate. If it had not been so, I would not have accepted the commission to protect these ideals."

"Second, I had self-discipline. It would have been easier to avoid torture by succumbing to my captive's interrogations. It would have been easier to assume helplessness by blaming an evil world. I could have rationalized myself into mental and physical paralysis. Quite simply, I could have just simply 'laid the bricks.' However, strict self-obedience gave me the ability to persevere."

"Third, I had pride. I was proud to know an omnipotent God. I was then and continue to be proud of my country and its heritage. I was proud of my family. I was proud of myself. So, I will ask again, who packed your parachute? Most importantly, whose parachute are you packing?"

# Chapter 30

## The Conclusion and the Debrief

I conclude in the manner I suggest concluding any significant meeting, planning session, training program, organizational milestone, crisis situation, business initiative, or even a book by tying a nice ribbon (metaphorically speaking) around that experience in the form of a formal debrief. But even with the best intentions, a meaningful debrief rarely occurs.

My experience in training and development includes a strong emphasis on the importance of the "Debrief." Preparing other trainers, commonly referred to as "Train the Trainer" programs, include three important steps (applicable to most organizational initiatives): (1) The Set Up (clear directions, rationale for and importance of a particular topic), (2) Management (ensuring participants pay attention and are engaged, creating an environment conducive to learning) and (3) The Debrief (applications, key points, lessons learned, action-plans, closure). While all three steps are equally important, a proper debrief is essential but again, rarely occurs.

The following is my Six-Step Debrief Model ©

## STEP 1: REVIEW

Here's what we've covered:

- Soft Skills: A Working Definition (*A compliment to and partner with Technical Skills, Soft Skills are a blend of credibility, likability & most importantly, authenticity.*)
- The Case for Soft Skills
- Building Cathedrals: The Power of Purpose (*Christopher Wren, the Three Bricklayers, a Cathedral as a metaphor, the redemptive qualities of a "Fire"*)
- Employee Engagement
- Bus Metaphor (Get the *Right people on the "Bus," the Right People in the Right Seats, and the Wrong People off the Bus*)
- What about the "Driver" of the bus? (*The leader*)
- Johari Window (*Arena, Blind Spot, Closet, Potential*)
- The Appreciation of Differences: Social Styles (*Drivers, Analyticals, Expressives, Amiables*)
- Stress Management (characteristics of Stress Resistant people)
- Emotional Intelligence

- Forgiveness & Reconciliation
- Coaching
- Seven Dynamics of Change
- Steps of Team Growth (*Form, Storm, Norm, Perform*)
- Situational Leadership/Management (*Directive, Coaching, Supporting, Delegation*)
- Readiness Levels
- The 12 Elements of Great Managing
- The Five Practices of Exemplary Leadership
- Be-Know-Do
- Culture-The Personality of Your Organization
- Customer Service: Back to the Basics
- Problem Solving/Action Planning
- Organizational Dynamics
- Soft Skills Strategies
- The Debrief

## STEP 2: LESSONS LEARNED

The most important three questions for any Debrief:

1. *What went well?*
2. *Where did we get stuck?*
3. *What should we do differently next time?*

## ADDITIONAL QUESTIONS

1. Overall, what are your general thoughts about Soft Skills?

2. As a result of reading Soft Skills Field Manual, has your perspective on Soft Skills changed? If so, please explain.

3. What topic most grabbed your attention?

4. What are your greatest Soft Skills?

5. What are your greatest Soft Skills growth areas?

6. Specifically, what is your personal improvement plan as it relates to Soft Skills?

7. What would you liked to have been covered in our seminar that wasn't?

8. What ideas do you have of enhancing Soft Skills within your organization?

## STEP 3: NEXT STEPS

- Soft Skills Training (*Soft Skills Boot Camp*) within your organization?

- Specific strategies for individual/organizational Soft Skills enhancement?

- Soft Skills organizational assessment opportunities? (Survey, Focus Groups, etc.)

- Other logical *Next Steps*?

- Would others in your organization benefit from reading and discussing Soft Skills Field Manual?

* *The agreed upon items in this step should be outlined in Step 4: Action Plan, below.*

## STEP 4: ACTION PLAN

## Action Plan

| WHAT | WHO | WHEN |
|------|-----|------|
|      |     |      |
|      |     |      |
|      |     |      |

## STEP 5: RECOGNITION

Mike Robbins, author of *Focus on the Good Stuff: The Power of Appreciation,* describes the important distinction between "Recognition" and "Appreciation." Recognition is positive feedback based on performance, results and outcomes. Recognition is finite, scarce and from an organizational delivered by a superior(s) in order to carry significant weight and/or merit. Recognition is good business and a key Soft Skill. In fact, a UC Berkeley study found that when people felt positively recognized for the work they did, there was a 23 percent increase in productivity.

Behavior is repeated to the extent it's reinforced, so it begs the question what behaviors are we most recognizing? Are we constantly running out to the shop floor delivering corrective action or are most visits to deliver a well deserved "pat on the back?" As parents, is the feedback we give to our children more corrective in nature or more encouraging and filled with praise for good behavior and habits? As Tom Peters, author of *In Search of Excellence*, is fond of saying, "Celebrate what you want to see more of!"

## STEP 6: APPRECIATION

Appreciation is closely related to Recognition. Appreciation is based on the value we place on another person. Appreciation is more expansive, more about people, less about what others do and more about who they are. In the same UC Berkeley study, when people reported feeling valued and cared for (*in addition to being recognized*) there was a 43 percent increase in productivity, a 20 percent increase! Additionally, when one expresses kindness and appreciation to another, and it's received, it raises the serotonin level in both people's brain!

"Appreciate" or risk losing good employees. A Department of Labor study asked employees the main reason for leaving a job and they found 64 percent saying they didn't feel appreciated or valued. One of my favorite Bible stories (Luke 17:11-19) is the one of Jesus healing the ten lepers. Only one disciple returned to show appreciation, which prompted Jesus to ask, "Were not all ten cleansed? Where are the other nine?"

I close by "returning" to say thank you for the time you've invested in Soft Skills and the trust you've placed in me, my experience and perspectives on a variety of topics. I sincerely appreciate you and your organization's investment in Soft Skills Field Manual and associated workshops. Appreciation may indeed be the ultimate Soft Skill and I challenge you to look for every opportunity to thank those who make a difference in your life, both personally and professionally.

Good luck, God Bless and God Speed!

April 2016

# Appendix

## SOFT SKILLS BOOT CAMP

While today's employees are technically competent, they often lack what is commonly referred to as "Soft Skills." Workplace skills such as communication, problem solving, customer service, teamwork and conflict resolution. They leave school knowing "Things" but not "People." They're good at the "What" but not so good with the "Who."

Greg Coker, author of *Building Cathedrals: The Power of Purpose* and *Soft Skills Field Manual*, has made a career of teaching senior level executives the fundamentals of individual and organizational effectiveness. Now, he takes these time-tested "Soft Skills" and shares them with you and your front-line!

Soft Skills Boot Camp is guaranteed to increase employee satisfaction while boosting productivity, engagement levels and customer loyalty. And it doesn't end after the workshop! Greg provides each participant the opportunity for ongoing one-on-one coaching on specific strategies covered in the workshop as well as customized solutions tailored for each person.

Workshop Outline (*customized for your organization*)

- Individual & Organization Effectiveness
- Employee Engagement
- Creativity, Project Management & Problem Solving
- Communication Excellence
- Emotional Intelligence
- Conflict Resolution
- Stress Management
- Organizational Change
- Managing & Leading
- Team Effectiveness
- Organization Dynamics/Politics
- Customer Loyalty

Building Cathedrals:
The Power of Purpose Series

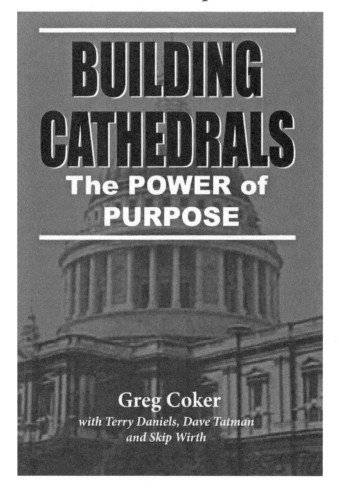

# The Speech - Motivational

*Building Cathedrals: The Power of Purpose* is based on a story that has been told for over 300 years – one that illustrates the most productive and successful people in life are those of purpose. And while many have heard a version of this apocryphal story, Greg Coker has traced the origin of this life-changing story to the world's most famous architect, Christopher Wren, who was commissioned to rebuild Saint Paul's Cathedral after the devastating London fire of 1666.

Greg captivates his readers as he enriches this story dissecting the leadership qualities of Christopher Wren and revisiting the fire of 1666 and its redemptive qualities, not only to London but in our personal lives as well. He introduces a powerful metaphor, a "Cathedral," as something that adds purpose to our lives, that drives our behavior, while encouraging us to not only find our "Cathedral," but to help and support others in finding their "Cathedral."

The "Bricklayers" in the story provide the backdrop for a rich discussion on employee engagement and the dynamics that occur in modern day organizations. The highlight of the keynote are personal stories of people who are building modern day "Cathedrals" and those who have experienced "personal fires." But like London, they were able to come out stronger, quicker, faster. Greg concludes with simple yet powerful examples of how we have the amazing power and the responsibility to touch and inspire others in a deep and meaningful way.

As a professional speaker, Greg travels the country delivering this powerful speech in an entertaining and inspirational style to Fortune 500 companies, government agencies, trade associations, civic organizations, colleges and universities. Greg's presentation, tailored especially for you and your organization, will inspire, motivate and move audiences through a range of emotions that ultimately results in everyone leaving with a renewed commitment to one's purpose and a clearer understanding of the "Cathedrals" that must be built, both personally and organizationally.

*Call Greg today at 270-223-8343 and schedule him for your next event!*

# The Workshop - Transformational

This powerful workshop, based on Greg's book and keynote speech, *"Building Cathedrals: The Power of Purpose"* is customized especially for you and your organization and is offered in both half-day and full-day sessions. While the book and the keynote speech are *motivational*, this workshop is *transformational*, focusing on seven keys areas guaranteed to take your company from a culture of "Bricklayers" to a culture of "Cathedral Builders":

- Leadership
- Engagement
- Culture
- Change Management
- Customer Loyalty
- Teamwork
- Communication

# Communication & Sales Excellence

It's simple. People buy on emotion; justify with fact. You buy that car because you connect with the salesperson; you trust her and you really like her. And then, you go home and google *Consumer Reports* as fast as you can so you can justify to your significant other why you bought that particular car! We buy from "whom" and not from "what." In short, it's about building rapport; it's about the relationship. It has more to do with EI (*emotional intelligence*) than with IQ. This "game changing" intervention can be delivered to your entire office staff in a workshop format or one-on-one in a coaching setting. Either way, your sales and referrals will increase, relationships will be strengthened and your negotiations more productive and profitable!

# Achieving Customer Loyalty

While there's no shortage of books, articles and even workshops on customer service, Greg takes a few very simple models and distills them down for immediate understanding and application. Greg uses the metaphors of "Building Cathedrals" versus "Laying Bricks" and relates them to achieving and maintaining customer loyalty for your organization. Powerful, memorable and immediately useful models such as the *Human-Business Model, Customer Report Card and Cycles of Service* are the highlight of this workshop. Let your competition continue to "Lay the Bricks" while Greg helps transform your company to a culture of "Cathedral Builders!"

# Strategic Planning

If you're looking for THE intervention to take your team and organization to the next level, THIS IS IT! This off-site session begins with the creation or revision of your team's mission and vision. From there, the focus is on identifying team strengths (*maximize*) and growth areas (*minimize/eliminate*). Greg will then guide you through the prioritization of growth areas and facilitate/coach your team through a practical problem-solving process. The result is a comprehensive action plan with timelines and individual/team accountabilities identified and committed to. Mission accomplished!

# Executive/Personal Coaching

Greg offers confidential and customized coaching working one-on-one with successful leaders assisting them in reaching even greater heights-by achieving positive, lasting change in behavior for themselves, their people and their organization. Greg's coaching has increased personal effectiveness, eliminated derailing behaviors and maximized peak performance for leaders across the United States. Organizational relationships, both vertical and horizontal, are the primary focus with external leveraging strategies presented as an opportunity to enhance leadership effectiveness and personal/organizational visibility.

## OBJECTIVES

- Provide real-time confidential coaching on issues and concerns confronting the participant.

- Establish long-term professional and career strategies, personalized and customized for the participant.

- Allow maximum flexibility and access that meet the participant's individualized needs.

- Provide maximum responsiveness.

## PARTICIPANT PROFILE

- Executives, new associates, performance program/corrective plan participants whose careers are worth salvaging.

- A need for independent, objective coaching on either business issues or personal style issues to enhance competence, performance, and/or image.

- A need for assistance with specific issues and/or with long-term plans, or for an objective sounding board to ensure validity of current behaviors and performance.

- A need for absolute confidential help at key times, requiring timely response with specific options for action.

## THE PROGRAM

- Telephone calls returned within 90 minutes, emails returned the same day; conventional mail, courier packages, and emails reviewed and replied to within 24 hours of receipt;

- Unlimited access. As many emails, phone calls, faxes and letters as desired, with responses provided as needed. 24 hours/7 days per week

- Sessions run in 30-day intervals.

# Organization Development - Taking the Pulse of your Organization

Unless the problem is crystal clear, you need a neutral, third party professional with the experience and expertise necessary to evaluate the situation from an objective point of view. You can rely on an accurate assessment and a workable solution with Greg Coker's five-phase approach:

- **PHASE 1** *Client-Consultant Contracting* (scheduling the initial meeting, exploring the problem/opportunity, client expectations, determining how best to get started)

- **PHASE 2** *Data Collection and Diagnosis* (determining who to involve in defining the problem; what methods will be used; specific data to be collected; timeframes)

- **PHASE 3** *Client Feedback and Decision to Act* (organizing information collected reducing to major themes as to best manage and understand while setting project goals and action steps)
- **PHASE 4** *Implementation*
- **PHASE 5** *Extension, Recycle or Termination* (evaluating the implementation phase, making a determination to extend the process to a larger segment of the organization)

**Greg Coker** is the founder of *The Cathedral Institute*, a full-service leadership development and consulting firm focusing on *Empowering People, Building Teams and Transforming Organizations*. He has over 25 years of experience as a senior level manager with three different fortune 500 companies, a government regulator and elected official.

Greg Coker is also a registered lobbyist advocating for clients at the local, state and federal level. His experience ranges from leading the training & development for over 80,000 employees to directing the governmental affairs and public relations at both the state and federal level. His clients include public education, business and industry, colleges and universities, nonprofit organizations and high performance individuals who benefit from his executive/life coaching.

Greg is the author of *"Building Cathedrals: The Power of Purpose"* and the *Soft Skills Field Manual*. He travels the country delivering keynote speeches and conducting workshops based on the principles of individual and organizational effectiveness, leadership, employee engagement, culture and purpose, which are the focal point of his books.

**Contact information**

Greg Coker

The Institute for Soft Skills

270-223-8343

www.softskillshq.com